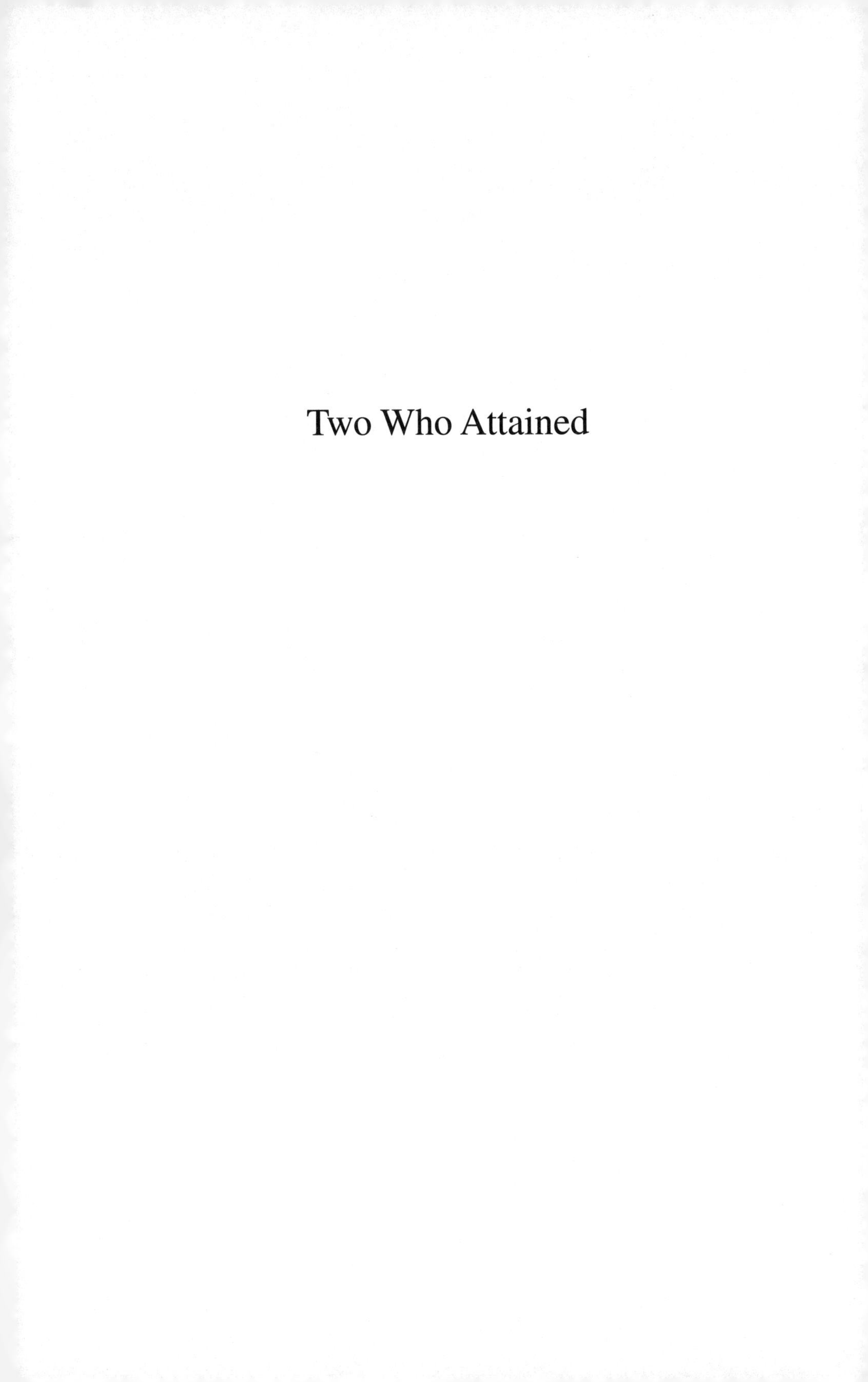

Two Who Attained

Two Who Attained

Twentieth-Century Muslim Saints

Sayyida Fatima al-Yashrutiyya

and

Shaykh Ahmad al-Alawi

Introduction and Translations by

Leslie Cadavid

FONS VITAE

First published in 2005 by
Fons Vitae
49 Mockingbird Valley Drive
Louisville, KY 40207
http://www.fonsvitae.com

Library of Congress Control Number: 2005927407

ISBN 1-887752-61-7

This book was typeset by Neville Blakemore, Jr.

Printed in Canada

Table of Contents

Foreword by Seyyed Hossein Nasr vii

Introduction xi

Extracts from the works of the Shaykh al-Alawi
- *Divine Graces* 1
- *Treatise on the Invocation of the Divine Name* 49
- Poetry from his *Diwān* 75

Extracts from the works of Fatima al-Yashrutiyya 107

Appendix: *Silsila* of the Shadhiliyya *Ṭarīqa* 225

Selected Bibliography 229

Translator's Biography 231

Index 233

Mostaganem

Acre

Foreword

Since the beginning of the study of Sufism in the West in the 19th century, most Western scholars looked upon it as a medieval phenomenon associated with the classical period of Islamic civilization and this attitude continued for the most part until the end of the first half of the 20th century. It is only in more recent decades that serious studies have become devoted in European languages to later Sufism and the knowledgeable Western public has come to realize that Sufism is a living tradition that has produced and continues to produce even in the age of the airplane and television outstanding saints and sages reminiscent of their "medieval" ancestors. When the late Martin Lings sent the text of his now classical work on Shaykh al-'Alawi, a *Sufi Saint of Twentieth Century*, for publication, the publisher sent it to A.J. Arberry, one of the British authorities on Sufism, for his comments. Dr. Lings told me that after reading the manuscript, Arberry stated how surprised he was that a figure who reminded him of the great classical medieval Sufis should have lived in the 20th century. The readers of this volume should no longer be surprised, for meanwhile not only Shaykh al-'Alawi but also some of the other 20th century Sufi luminaries have become known in the West as a result of a number of studies devoted to them.

The present volume deals with the works of two Sufi figures, belonging to the last century, both from the Shadhiliyyah Order, Shaykh al-'Alawi himself and Sayyidah Fatimah Yashrutiyyah, a remarkable Sufi saint who was born and brought up in Palestine and later lived and died in Lebanon but who, in contrast to Shaykh al-'Alawi, has not been studied or translated extensively into English until now. Although many of Shaykh al-'Alawi's works have been rendered into French and some into English, the present selection is a precious addition to the corpus of his writings available in European languages. As for Sayyidah Fatimah Yashrutiyyah, her works are especially precious as examples of writings of Sufi women and of contemporary feminine spirituality in Islam.

I was born too late to have the possibility of meeting Shaykh al-'Alawi in this world, although the deepest bonds connect me to him and his spiritual reality. I did however, have the singular honor of meeting Sayyidah Fatimah more than once in Beirut in the 1960's and a profound bond of friendship developed between us. When I first met her, she was already biologically old but had the presence of a young, beautiful woman. Ibn 'Arabi has written of one of his female spiritual teachers in Andalusia who was very old but appeared like a young beauty. The same was true of Sayyidah Fatimah. She exuded a presence of remarkable gentleness, refinement and humility combined with a beauty marked by the luminosity of sincerity and receptivity of and transparency before the Truth. She exemplified on an exalted level female sanctity whose supreme exemplar in Islam is the daughter of the Prophet, Fatimah, after whom she was named. One sensed in the presence of Sayyidah Fatimah Yashrutiyyah a distinct perfume of feminine spirituality in addition to the ubiquitous *barakah* which surrounds those devoted to the remembrance of God.

Some twenty years ago, as an advisor to the Western Spirituality Series, I suggested to Leslie Cadavid that she translate a selection of the writings of these two remarkable 20th century Sufi saints and sages, Shaykh al-'Alawi and Sayyidah Fatimah Yashrutiyyah in a volume, for that series. It is a source of joy to see that after two decades, this work has now been achieved. Fons Vitae must be thanked for publishing this work and the translator must be highly congratulated for having made such precious writings available in an authentic and elegant language to the English reading public. Besides its innate value, this volume is important for bringing to light the nature of Sufism as a living reality which makes available, in this age of spiritual darkness, an authentic spiritual path to the One, making it possible to quote the title of one of Sayyidah Fatimah's major works, the *Journey to the Truth.*

Seyyed Hossein Nasr
Bethesda, Maryland
July 2005

A note on the transliterations and footnotes contained in this work: we have followed the convention of applying diacritical marks to titles of works and Arabic terms, but not to proper names or places. Where the footnote indicates a quote from the Quran, it is understood to be such when only the chapter and verses are listed, e.g., LXI, 63.

The selections in this book are taken from two Muslim authors of the twentieth century; both represent Islam in its esoteric dimension of Sufism, and both are regarded as saints by the Muslims of today. In order to fully understand their writings it is necessary for the reader to have some familiarity with the fundamental principles of the Sufi doctrine and method.

Sufism is the heart of Islam and has as its goal the realization of the oneness of God, formulated by the first *shahāda* or testimony of faith. This realization, however, is not to be restricted to the mental plane, but is to penetrate to the heart and the inner substance of man. It is thus a way of realizing in the most profound depths of the human soul the meaning of revealed doctrines. Whereas exoterism demands of men conformity to the will of God on a more or less horizontal plane, esoterism adds a further dimension of height and depth to this conformity of faith. It has been described in a *ḥadīth*[1] as *iḥsān*, which means that one should worship God "as if you saw Him." It is this direct experiencing of God that distinguishes Sufism from exoteric Islam. The first *shahāda* contains the doctrine of the transcendent unity of God—"there is no divinity save God"—while the second *shahāda*—"Muhammad is the messenger of God"—bears witness to the divine immanence, to the Logos which is part human and part divine by his receptivity to the revelation of the Word of God, the Quran. Through conformity to the Muhammadan norm or *Sunna*[2] the Sufi realizes the divine presence immanent in the heart expressed in the *ḥadīth*, "Neither My heavens nor My earth can contain Me, but the heart of My believing slave contains Me."

All of the doctrines pertaining to this esoteric dimension come from the Quran or the sayings of the Prophet, for these can be interpreted in various ways, from the most exoteric and literal meaning to one that is esoteric or symbolic. There are also instances where even the literal meaning is clearly closer to estorism than exoterism, as in the verse: "Unto God belong the east and the west, and wheresoever ye turn, there is the Face of God. Verily God is All-Embracing, All-Knowing."[3] The Sufi strives to truly see God everywhere; thus all of the exoteric dogmas have for him an inner meaning. For him the *Sharīᶜa*, or Islamic Law, is the vehicle of the *Ḥaqīqa,* or inner Reality, and opens onto it. Sufism thus enjoys a certain independence with regard to forms by virtue of its intellectual sovereignty. These Sufi saints understood the meaning and symbolism of forms and would never advise an exoteric Muslim to neglect them. They themselves adhered to the essential and required forms of exoteric Islam, but with an esoteric understanding of forms so that they became a primordial and universal support for the invocatory way. The famous example of Al-Hallaj saying, "I am the Truth" (*Ana al-Ḥaqq*) is explained by the Shaykh al-Alawi as a case of someone who lacked the inward station of sobriety (*ṣaḥw*) and thus gave unrestrained expression to their sublime state. Abu al-Hasan al-Shadhili, founder of the Shadhili *ṭarīqa* (spiritual brotherhood) once spoke to God in a vision saying, "Shall I tell the people of Thine infinite mercy, so that they will never again bow down to Thee in prayer?" He spoke from a position of intimacy (*uns*) and sanctity (*wilāya*), and he was thus freed from the restraints of forms.

Both the Shaykh al-Alawi and Fatima al-Yashrutiyya are representatives of the Shadhili *ṭarīqa* founded in Egypt by Abu al-Hasan al-Shadhili in the thirteenth century. Several of the authors quoted in the selections, such as Ibn Ata Allāh and Ahmad Zarruq share the same spiritual lineage.[4] The Shadhili *ṭarīqa* distinguished itself by initiating people who by and large kept their professions and positions in society and did not leave the world to don the coarse woolen garment characteristic of some Sufis of the day. They integrated their lives into the path and were, although in the world, not of it.

The method of the Sufi way is essentially the invocation, or "remembrance" of God (*dhikr Allāh*) by means of His Supreme Name or one of His other divine names. The practice of this invocation can be traced back to the Quran in such verses as "…hold fast and invoke God much…,"[5] "remember Me, I will remember you,"[6] and "verily, the remembrance of God is of all things the greatest."[7] This repetition of God's name encompasses, for the Sufis, all other acts of worship. This is the recurring theme of the writings of both authors. Titus Burckhardt eloquently explains the sense of the word "remembrance" (*dhikr*) for the Sufis as follows: "Deflected from its true centre, which has its roots in the Eternal, the consciousness of the average man is as if imprisoned in a kind of dream or state of forgetfulness (*ghafla*). This is why man must be 'reminded' (of That which he has 'forgotten'), and this is the reason for what is known as *dhikr*, which the Sufi must practice in a large variety of ways, and which may be translated as 'remembrance,' 'mention,' 'invocation.' *Dhikr* is closely related to the 'prayer of the heart' of the Hesychasts of Eastern Christianity.

"Since the goal of the mystical path is the transcending of the empirical ego, it cannot be embarked upon without grace (*tawfīq*), nor can it be followed without the help of a spiritual master (*shaykh* or *murshid*) who has himself traversed it, and without the spiritual influence or benediction that he confers on the disciple."[8] This last remark explains why, without initiation from a master whose spiritual lineage is traced back to the Prophet Muhammad, a man cannot receive the special grace that emanates from the Muhammadan *baraka*, or blessing. Without going into further detail, these are the central characteristics and aspects of Sufism. The Shaykh al-Alawi has explained all this and more in his work *al-Minaḥ al-Quddūsiyya*, and from Sayyida Fatima al-Yashrutiyya[9] we have a section on Sufism as well. The Shaykh al-Alawi precedes Fatima al-Yashrutiyya in time, having been born in 1869 in Mostaganem, Algeria. Sayyida Fatima's father, the Shaykh al-Yashruti was born in 1791 in Tunisia, but was by 1869 already in Acre, Palestine, having established his *zāwiya*[10] there. Thus it is doubtful that these two Shadhili masters ever met one another, although the Shaykh al-Yashruti lived until 1899. We know that the Shaykh al-Alawi traveled to Syria and established *zāwiyas* in Gaza, Jaffa, and Feluja, but there is no mention of this in Sayyida Fatima's works.

The Shaykh al-Alawi's *zāwiya* in Mostaganem attracted some thousands of aspirants during his lifetime. He had attached himself at an early age to Shaykh Muhammad al-Buzidi, after several meetings with the latter and after realizing the greatness of his spiritual station. This Shaykh ordered him to practice the invocation of the name *Allāh*, and guided him through the stages of the path until he attained his goal. He was then able to guide others, and of this wrote: "The path which I have just described as being that of my master is the one that I have followed in my own spiritual guidance, leading my own followers along it, for I have found it the nearest of paths that lead to God."[11] When the Shaykh al-Alawi had achieved realization of God and saw through the illusory nature of the world, his Shaykh ordered him to return to the lessons of theology which he had been attending previously. When he resumed the lessons he realized everything had changed for him, however. In his words, "Another result of the invocation was that I understood more than the literal sense of the text. In a word, there was no comparison between the understanding which I now had and that which I had before, and its scope went on increasing, until when anyone recited a passage from the Book of God my wits would jump to solve the riddle of its meaning with amazing speed at the very moment of recitation. But when this took hold of me and became almost second nature, I was afraid that I should become altogether under the sway of its imperious and persistent impulsion, so I took to writing down what my inward thoughts dictated to me by way of interpretation of the Book of God, and I was so much under its sway that I brought them out in a strange and abstruse form. This is what led me to begin commentary on *al-Murshid al-Muᶜīn* in an attempt to stop myself from falling into a still more abstruse manner of expression. God be praised that this did in fact help to stem the onslaughts of that surge of thoughts which I had tried by every means to stop and could not, and my mind came near to being at rest."[12] The above-mentioned work by Ibn Ashir (d. 1631) is his *Guide to the Essentials of Religious Knowledge*, containing in rhymed form the doctrine and laws of Islam, which every new *faqīr*[13] should know. The Shaykh al-Alawi's esoteric commentary on this work is his *Divine Graces (al-Minaḥ al-Quddūsiyya)*, from which we have chosen selections from the Book of Doctrine and the Book of Prayer. In it he gives the inner significance of the exoteric rites of the religion, including in addition to what we have selected, the pilgrimage, almsgiving, the fast, and the Sufi path or *ṭarīqa*. The work was written, as he has described above, because of his overflowing thoughts and piercing discernment of the inner reality behind the literal words of the text. It was often given to new disciples to read to help them understand the esoteric significance of the rites of Islam. As such it is one of his most important works. It was completed while his Shaykh was still living, that is, prior to 1909, but was later revised for publication.

Our other selection from the Shaykh's writings is the *Treatise on the Invocation of the Divine Name* (*al-Qawl al-Muᶜtamad fī Mashrūᶜiyya al-Dhikr bi al-Ism al-Mufrad*), written about 1927. This second work is different in tone and flavor from the first, having been written in defense of attacks by a legalistic scholar upon his Order for their practice of the invocation. In it the Shaykh al-Alawi, knowing the mentality of his adversary, corroborates his defense with numerous examples from the Quran, the traditions of the Prophet, and other legal scholars and well-known saints. The defense was first published as a serial in *al-Balāgh al-Jazāʾiri*, a journal of the Alawi *ṭarīqa* which the Shaykh had established to educate his disciples and the public at large regarding the false ideas and ways of thinking prevalent at the time. He hoped by it to engender a spiritual revival in the people, and to defend Sufism against the narrow-minded legalistic religious scholars who often opposed its practices. *Al-Qawl al-Muᶜtamad* was written in response to a visit he had from someone, who complained that the invocation of the Divine Name by itself was grammatically incorrect and therefore without meaning. Since the treatise was originally printed in serial form, it is inevitable that there be a certain amount of repetition; nevertheless, it contains a defense of the invocation and Sufism that any Sufi master could well employ today. The arguments are direct, logical, and so well supported by quotes from irrefutable sources that one imagines his opponent having felt left with little, if anything, upon which to stand. Finally, we have included selections from his *Diwān*.

The Shaykh al-Alawi was often under attack by modernists and so-called religious reformers. Algeria was occupied by the French, and many Muslims found that the only way to cope with colonization was to take up western ways of dress and lifestyle, thereby abandoning their religion, and it was against this that he fought without cease. The Shaykh died in 1934 at the age of fifty-five, and by the end of his life is said to have had over one hundred thousand disciples. The following account, written by Frithjof Schuon, an eminent authority on comparative religion and spirituality, conveys an unforgettable image of this great master: "The idea which is the secret and the inner determination of every traditional form is too subtle and profound to be realized with equal intensity by all who breathe its atmosphere; it is thus all the more precious to come into contact with a messenger who represents the spirituality of one of those worlds which the modern West fails to understand. One could compare the encounter with one of these messengers to meeting, in the middle of the twentieth century, a medieval saint or semitic patriarch; such was the impression I had of one of the greatest Sufi masters of our time, the Shaykh al-Hajj Ahmad abu al-Abbas ibn Moustafa ibn Alawi, also known as the Shaykh al-Alawi, who passed away some months ago at Mostaganem.

"Dressed in a brown jallaba and white turban—with his silver-gray beard, his eyes of a visionary, and his long hands whose gestures seemed to be weighed down by the flow of his *baraka*, he exhaled something of the pure, archaic ambiance of Sayyidna Ibrahim al-Khalil.[14] He spoke in a subdued, gentle voice, a voice of splintered crystal, letting his words drop fragment by fragment; there was a detached, resigned tone in that voice, and it seemed as if the thoughts that it transmitted were no more than very fragile and transparent exteriorizations of an intelligence that was too conscious of itself to become dispersed in the flow of the contingent. His eyes, like two sepulchral lamps, seemed to see but one and the same reality in forms—that of the Infinite—or perhaps they saw in their outer shell but one and the same nothingness. His look was very direct, almost hard in its enigmatic immobility, yet full of charity. Often, his half-closed eyes would suddenly widen as if astonished or captivated by some marvelous sight. The rhythm of the singing, the dances, and the ritual chants seemed to vibrate ceaselessly within him; at times his head would rock rhythmically to and fro, while his soul was plunged in the inexhaustible mysteries of the Divine Name, hidden in the *dhikr*, the Remembrance.... He gave an impression of unreality, so distant, closed, and elusive was he in his entirely abstract simplicity. He was surrounded at once with the veneration due to saints, leaders, the old and the dying.

"What was his 'islam,' his 'abandon' to the divine Reality that becomes fatality when our own reality appears to leave it outside of Itself? It was perfection by the absence of imperfection, knowledge by the absence of ignorance. No act, no superfluous assertion, not even the desire to acquire a particular merit could disturb the equilibrium of that attitude of islam. It was in itself its own merit. One could no longer distinguish between effort and reward, sowing and reaping, in that equilibrium where the circle came closer and closer to the central point, Allah...."[15]

***

Sayyida Fatima al-Yashrutiyya was born in 1891, the daughter of the Shadhili Shaykh al-Yashruti whose *zāwiya* was in Acre, Palestine. As one of his few surviving children, Sayyida Fatima was the object of much of his affection and attention. At the age of two he began to take her with him to attend meetings of theologians and Sufis. She was evidently gifted, for when the Shaykh died in 1899 at the venerable age of one hundred and eight, she was a child of eight, yet she resolved to undertake the search for the knowledge that she had begun to taste and took it upon herself to read as many books as she could find on all aspects of Sufism and Islam. She continued these studies throughout the greater part of her life, and used to meet regularly with scholars and Sufis throughout the Middle East. It was certainly exceptional for a woman living in the early part of the twentieth century to meet thus with men and converse freely on various scholarly topics, but this can be explained in part by her exceptional gifts in the fields of learning and also in part by the fact that she was already well acquainted with the scholars of the day as a child and simply continued to keep up her contact with them. It is likely that it was as Hasan al-Basri is said to have related of Rabia al-Adawiyya: "I passed one whole night and day with Rabia speaking of the Way and the Truth, and it never passed through my mind that I was a man nor did it occur to her that she was a woman."[16]

Sayyida Fatima never married, nor does she mention any possibilities of marriage. This, too, was unusual and can perhaps be explained by her wholehearted devotion to the pursuit of knowledge and spiritual realization which took precedence over all else in her life.

The Yashruti *ṭarīqa* is a branch of the Shadhili *ṭarīqa* founded by Abu al-Hasan al-Shadhili. The Shaykh al-

Yashruti's master was the Shaykh al-Madani, and his master was the Shaykh al-Arabi al-Darqawi. The Yashruti order has many adherents throughout Palestine, Lebanon, and Syria, as well as in East Africa and even as far as South America. Sayyida Fatima wrote that the *ṭarīqa* spread to "Zanzibar and its coasts, the Comoro islands, Madagascar, Kenya, New Guinea, and Tanganyika. Throughout this region *zāwiyas* were built by the followers of the noble *ṭarīqa* and by our brethren in God."[17]

It is clear that although more than one Shaykh was elected to succeed the Shaykh al-Yashruti during Sayyida Fatima's lifetime, it was she who carried the *baraka* (blessing) of the order and she was, moreover, authorized to initiate others into it. Visiting disciples were interested in meeting her above everyone else and an acquaintance who knew her related to me that on one occasion some visiting African disciples lifted her onto their shoulders out of joy and reverence for her. She was, according to all accounts, very beautiful. Even when she was in her eighties her inner radiance shone forth, making her seem like a young woman. Jean-Louis Michon, a Swiss architect and Islamic scholar, met Sayyida Fatima in the late 70s in Beirut. He recounted that the meeting was "marvelous, she was nearly 80, without a wrinkle. A radiant face like a young girl, full of life yet very serene." One is reminded of Ibn Arabi, who was taught by a woman saint named Fatima in Cordoba. He related that in spite of her great age, she possessed all the beauty of a young girl. Ibn Arabi accorded women a very high position and saw them as a manifestation of the mercy (*raḥma*) of God. He is certainly not the only man in Islam to venerate women in this way. Throughout history the Muslim world has known saintly women whose *baraka* has survived down to the present. Fatima, daughter of the

Prophet, is one to whom some Muslims turn to for intercession; she has been given the honorific title of virgin (*al-baṭūl*), referring to her great purity of soul, for in her life she bore the famous Hasan and Husayn. Our Sayyida Fatima al-Yashrutiyya was named after none other than this great woman of early Islam.

Rabia al-Adawiyya, who we mentioned earlier, is probably the most outstanding example of a veritable master of the Sufi path of Love. For her, love for God is the motive behind every act, and her most famous and oft-quoted words are: "I have not served God from fear of Hell, for I should be like a wretched hireling, if I did it from fear; nor from love of Paradise, for I should be a bad servant if I served for the sake of what was given, but I have served Him only for the love of Him and desire for Him."[18] The love spoken of here is the highest station of the mystic and coincides, in essence, with the station of gnosis. Ibn Arabi in like manner has said: "My heart has opened to every form; it is a pasture for gazelles, a cloister for Christian monks, a temple for idols, the Kaaba for the pilgrim, the tables of the Torah and the book of the Quran. I practice the religion of Love; in whatsoever directions its caravans advance, the religion of Love shall be my religion and my faith."

The use of the word "love" here is explained by Frithjof Schuon thus: "Here it is not a question of *maḥabba* (love) in the psychological or methodological sense but of truth that is lived and of divine 'attraction.' Here 'love' is opposed to 'forms' which are envisaged as 'cold' and as 'dead.' St. Paul also says that 'the letter killeth, but the spirit maketh alive.' 'Spirit' and 'love' are here synonymous."[19] One could interpret the meaning of love as Rabia has used it in like manner, and thus it becomes the supreme state of union with the Spirit, where all individuality has melted away and there remains only consciousness of God in His Essence. The gnostics, of whom the Shaykh al-Alawi is an example, express this station differently. They say that the self-evidentness of God, being like the sun, banishes all ignorance and thus all separation from Him, so that the individual ceases to exist and only God exists in its place. Whatever the manner of expression, the stations spoken of are the same.

The fact that so many scholars from both east and west went to visit Sayyida Fatima during her lifetime demonstrates the importance of her position in the world of Islam and Sufism. Indeed, her education in the realm of law, jurisprudence, theology, and Sufism was unrivalled for a woman of the twentieth century. The essay that she wrote in 1973 as a contribution to a conference in Houston, Texas has the ring of authority of someone who was both a learned scholar and profound thinker. In it she wrote: "The salvation of the soul and the attainment of knowledge of God is the legacy of purification. We maintain, therefore, that Sufism is the most noble and excellent of all the sciences because its subject is the knowledge of God (may He be praised and exalted!), His names, His qualities, and His deeds. While the virtues of acquiring knowledge in all fields are the duty of every Muslim, every branch of knowledge derives its honor from the level of that which it seeks to know and the fruits thereof. The study of the physical world as the handiwork of God Almighty is a natural and noble activity of man. It is obvious that man's finite intellect, if he is on the right path, is drawn and moves toward the Infinite. Thus the knowledge of God is more noble and complete than the knowledge of anything else knowable, and the fruits of it lead to felicity in this world and the next. Moreover, the seeker of knowledge is usually affected by that which he seeks and gradually his life and soul are molded by the qualities and attributes of the 'known.' Thus the knowledge of every attribute of God leads to a spiritual state."[20]

Sayyida Fatima died in 1978 in Beirut at the age of eighty-seven. She has left us with four books: *Journey on the Path of Truth* (*Riḥla ila al-Ḥaqq*), *My Journey on the Path of Truth* (*Masirati fī Tarīq al-Ḥaqq*), *Gifts of the Truth* (*Muwāhib al-Ḥaqq*), and *Perfumes of the Truth* (*Nafaḥāt al-Ḥaqq*). It is rare to find among the Sufis a woman who wrote of her path to God for later generations to read. Indeed, few if any women wrote at all; for the most part we must content ourselves with later writings about them by their followers and admirers. This rarity makes Sayyida Fatima's writings all the more valuable. In *Journey to the Truth* we find the life story of her father, recounting his travels from his home in Tunisia, where he was born in 1791, to his final residence in Acre, Palestine. His life spanned more than a century and saw great changes in the lives and surroundings of the Muslim world as so-called 'progress' and westernization crept in. Sayyida Fatima herself would perhaps never have written her first work were it not for the fact that several disciples and friends had requested it of her, and she was then divinely inspired to write. This book and the rest of her works were written primarily for the other disciples of the Yashrutiyya order and not so much for outsiders unfamiliar with the world of the *ṭarīqa*. In her works she is full of praise for the Sufi way, and she explains what it is and how one must follow it, depending on the predisposition of the soul. She also defends the invocation of the Divine Name, using arguments from the Quran as does the Shaykh al-Alawi. The last work she wrote was *My Journey on the Path of Truth*, which contains the story of her life as well as descriptions of many members of her family. *Gifts of the Truth* and *Perfumes of the Truth* tell about life in the *ṭarīqa* and record numerous miracles which graced the Shaykh and other disciples. Certainly the most important of her works are the first two and it is almost exclusively from these that selections have been taken.

The Shaykh al-Alawi and Sayyida Fatima al-Yashrutiyya give a taste of the world of the Shadhili *ṭarīqa*, in different modes and different levels, but with an underlying theme of concentration on the oneness of God. Both witnessed their traditional world begin to fall apart. Both were beacons of light to those who clung to the Path in spite of the trials of the modern world; both proved that the Shadhili *ṭarīqa* was still very much alive in the twentieth century. When asked about the strength of the Yashruti following in the 1970s, Sayyida Fatima said, "Ours is a materialistic age, but there *are* those who follow the Way. Good men are always in the minority. But that does not matter. Numbers are not what count. One person can be worth more than thousands. Many thousands are not worth one good man." This is perhaps not surprising, for it is said that Abu al-Hasan al-Shadhili was told in a vision that his Order would remain "until the end of time."

Notes

1. A saying of the Prophet Muhammad, either in his own words or in the words of God through him, in which case it is called a *ḥadīth qudsi*.

2. The model or example given by the Prophet Muhammad as related by oral tradition (*ḥadīth*). Adherence to the Sunna is necessary as "No one shall meet God who has not first met the Prophet" (*ḥadīth*).

3. II, 115.

4. See *Silsila*, p. 225.

5. V, 45.

6. II, 152.

7. XXIX, 45.

8. *Fez, City of Islam*, trans. by William Stoddart, p. 130.

9. The term "*sayyida*" is an honorific title meaning "lady" and will be used henceforth when referring to Fatima al-Yashrutiyya, just as the term "*shaykh*" is used for the Shaykh al-Alawi.

10. Literally "corner," used to denote the Sufi meeting-houses and living quarters.

11. Martin Lings, *A Sufi Saint of the Twentieth Century*, p. 56.

12. Ibid, p. 58.

13. Literally "poor," "in need," signifying the Sufi disciple who is in need of God.

14. Abraham.

15. *Cahiers du Sud*, Aout-Septembre, 1935, p. 135.

16. Attar, *Tadhkirāt al-Awliyā*ʾ, p. 65.

17. *Riḥla ila al-Ḥaqq*, pp. 257–8.

18. Margaret Smith, *Rabia the Mystic*, p. 102.

19. *Understanding Islam*, p. 42.

20. *Traditional Modes of Contemplation and Action*, pp. 452–3.

The *zāwiya* of Ahmad ben Mustapha al-Alawi (1869-1934).

Extracts from *Divine Graces* (*al-Minaḥ al-Qudussiya*) By The Shaykh al-Alawi

In the Name of God, the Merciful, the Compassionate

Know that this knowledge of the Divine is favored above all others; to have an understanding of it is better than all else, and no one denies it save he who is cut off from its blessings. One may at some time be able to do without other forms of knowledge, but one cannot do without this knowledge at any time, and no one claims to be able to, save the ignorant man who is deprived of the taste of union; and he who turns away from something is thereby put far from it. Al-Ghazali often used to refer to the two verses by Abu al-Fath al-Busti (may God have mercy on them both!) which are as follows: "O servant of the body, how you strive in its service! And seek profit through things of error. You have a duty to your soul, so perfect its happiness. For you are by virtue of the soul, not the body, a man." We can see by these words that this knowledge is the noblest of all, for its nobility derives from the nobility of the known, and its power derives from the power of that with which it is associated, namely the Eternal itself. God possesses a nobility above all things, and all other realms of knowledge are but slaves and handmaidens to it. This is demonstrated by the words: "O you who hasten, seeking knowledge. All knowledge is a slave to spiritual knowledge. You seek to know the law in order to act correctly, while you ignore the One who revealed all wisdom."

The one referred to these verses should be a slave in service of the knowledge of the folk.[1] This knowledge, which is the subject of this work, is acquired through experience of the evidence of the Real, unlike other forms of knowledge obtained through indications and proofs. Beyond the clear proof there is no other. Indirect knowledge is not equal to direct experience.

The wise among the Sufis are divided into two types; those who are guided by its laws, and those who guide (others) to its way. In all other forms of knowledge disputes and arguments arise between its supporters and those who oppose it, and the leaders of various groups may become separated from the main body and form their own school. This could not happen with the Sufis, for their knowledge is on a level far above dissension and turmoil. Sidi Umar ibn al-Farid said: "How many arguments are held among those in details of law learned, while there is not, among the enamored of the Beloved, any dissent." Iz al-Din ibn Abd al-Salam (may God have mercy on him!) said, "The folk, that is, the Sufis, adhere to those rules of the law (*sharīᶜa*) which can be destroyed neither in this world or the next, while others have settled for the outward forms (*rusūm*) alone." Proofs showing the truth of the above are to be found in the miracles they have performed, in their guidance of men, and in their words of wisdom and counsel, such that those who keep company with them benefit in a way they could not with the pure exoterists. Al-Nawawi, in his commentary on the Shafii school of law (may God be pleased with both!) related that the latter said, "In keeping the company of Sufis I have benefited by two of their sayings: 'Time is a sword; if you do not cut it, it will cut you,' and 'If you do not occupy your soul (*nafs*) with good works, it will occupy you with evil works.'" Thus observe, brother, how this great imam testified with seriousness and *ijtihād*[2] in favor of the Sufis. Shaykh al-Shirani (may God be pleased with him!) said: "Observe how al-Shafii reserved these words for the Sufis and not for anyone else, showing that they enjoyed favor above others; if this were not so, he would not have limited his statement to them alone, but would have included the doctors of the law with whom he studied."

We can see that this knowledge is that of the sincere believer; he who is granted a portion of it is of those who have attained to a station of proximity far above those who are simply on the right side of the truth.[3] What happiness is his who attains to the highest intimacy with this knowledge! And what sorrow waits for the one who, out of ignorance and malice, opposes its adherents, contending with them about their knowledge, or quarreling with them over what does not concern him. This is all the more foolish when he argues with one who has no wish to argue with him. A wise man has said, "Whoever shows aggression towards one who is not opposing him will be punished by affliction." Brother, you are obliged to think well of God and His pious servants, particularly those who follow this path, for false talk in opposition to them is a deadly poison, may God protect us and all believers from this!

Concerning how one word may have several meanings:

Know that the folk only understand the speech of creatures in terms of its relation to God and do not allow their own ego to interpret it. This is required by their station. Do not, therefore, think it strange, brother, if they understand from a word a meaning that is different from its apparent one. This is but evidence of the nobility of their station and the exaltation of their degree, for they understand matters in God. The Sufis declare that such understanding in God is proportionate to one's station before Him, and they are united in saying that a single word, which refers to a specific meaning, can have, for the worshipper, innumerable possible meanings and an inexhaustible number of subtle and rare nuances. They say that a disciple must hear things only through God and His Messenger, or through that which brings him nearer to them. A word may be outwardly plain, but the realized man can obtain something enlightening from it by means of symbolism or allusion.

The folk, although participating with others in outward utterances, differ from them in their intentions, just as they participate with others in the act of looking at an object while perceiving something different. In the same way, they participate in listening along with others but what they hear is different. The Most High has said, "They are watered with the same water. And we have made some of them to excel others in fruit."[4] The Sufi may hear what others cannot, and he takes only the best of what he hears. Of these men God has said, "Those who hear words and follow the best thereof. Such are those who God hath guided, such are men of understanding."[5]

Glory be to the One who guided them and made them draw near to Him, bestowing upon them of His bounty, until they came to take their knowledge and actions from their Lord. They hear what the rest of creation is deaf to, and perceive what the rest of creation is blinded to. Their bodies reside with us while their spirits are with the Lord of Truth. One of them has said, "My heart with my Beloved resides, in intimate discourse with Him, while you have but my tongue."

God never takes under His protection an ignorant saint without granting him knowledge. He begins by teaching him about Himself and then teaches him His wisdom. As for the other domains of knowledge, they are not requirements for true sanctity but are rather requirements for human perfection. There are sciences such as grammar, morphology, rhetoric, explanations on various topics, and linguistics which most Sufis have little knowledge of, on account of the high degree of their fervor, the nobility of their stations before God, and the richness of their knowledge of Him. The Prophet (peace be upon him!) said regarding them: "He who is not enriched by the knowledge of God is a miserable man." It is not to be seen as a defect in them if they neglect those sciences in favor of the rules of worship, for that would be to strive for a lower perfection while neglecting true perfection, as Sidi Ahmad ibn Ajiba al-Maghribi said (may God be pleased with him!): "Righteousness of the tongue without righteousness of the heart is corruption and error. And righteousness of heart without righteousness of the tongue is perfection that yet lacks perfection. And righteousness of both heart and tongue is the perfection of perfections." What good is there in righteousness of the tongue without righteousness of the heart also? Have you seen the one who contents himself with words, while possessing no spiritual station, or who is content with speaking and does not act upon his words? Is the tongue not in need of faith? And are teachings not in need of direct experience?

On the words, "And pray and ask for peace upon Muhammad, his family, companions, and followers."

Prayer among the folk is, in essence, divine illumination. This is to say, when God, blessed and exalted, reveals Himself to one of His slaves, choosing him above others and causing him to enter into His Presence, at times revealing

Himself and at times hidden, His slave becomes aflame with longing for Him. Each time He appears to him his fears are calmed and his heart is put at rest. This grace is given only to prophets and to the greatest of the saints, and thus none of us are permitted to ask of God that He pray upon anyone other than His prophets, the elite of His saints, and those who are of a station or rank that is only enjoyed by the greatest of sages. "Prayer" here means "illumination" or "blessings" if it comes from God, and if not, then it has the meaning of a personal prayer. It is as if I said, "O God! Reveal Thyself to Muhammad and to his family." If it had not this meaning, the Prophet (peace and blessings be upon him!) would not have desired it and ordered us to pray thus at all times and in all circumstances. By this one gains illumination of the Essence so that Its names and attributes are revealed in the world through forms. When this is the state of things most of the time, then he (the slave) can scarcely bear to hear of anything other than God. The Prophet, upon him be blessing and peace, said, "There is a time when nothing suffices me save my Lord." This time is the time of the blessing of God upon the Prophet, of His illumination upon him. He never ceased asking God for this illumination, and his community now asks for it on his behalf and will continue to do so until the Day of Judgment. If the word 'prayer' had meant simply 'mercy' he would have been content with it and needed no more, according to God's words, "And We sent you not save as a mercy to the worlds."[6] As for the bestowal of peace by God upon His servant, this confers certitude and strength in the divine illumination he is receiving, and thus man must not only ask for blessings (*al-ṣalāt*), but must also ask for peace (*al-salām*). Peace cannot come before blessings, for this peace is a fixed and permanent quality granted by the state of illumination and realization. God, exalted and blessed, may bestow blessings upon some of His slaves while withholding peace from them. This causes their illumination to be characterized by violence, and at times fear, and inward commotion and agitation. As their anxiety increases so do their cries for help. They divulge their state to those who are not of their spiritual station, and as a result are accused of speaking falsehoods and judged as deviators from the straight path. This is because they are receiving only *ṣalāt* from God. If the Exalted wishes to preserve them and to preserve others through them, He follows His *ṣalāt* with *salām*, and then their fears are calmed and their path straightened so that they reside outwardly among men but inwardly in God, combining the two poles in their person. Two worlds governed by the wisdom of the two stations. These are the heirs of the prophets on account of their noble station. They speak of the states of drunkenness (*sukr*) and sobriety (*ṣaḥw*), of extinction (*fanāʾ*) and subsistence (*baqāʾ*), and shed light on the aspects where drunkenness alludes to the blessing of God upon them, and sobriety, to the peace which follows upon drowning in the presence of their Lord.

Know that the prophets (upon them be blessings and peace!) are distinguished in that they combine in their person both the blessings and peace of God, at times given all at once to them, at times given gradually. As for the saints, (may God be pleased with them!) some of them are characterized by blessings rather than by peace, and this station is known as that of drunkenness. Within this group there are those who return to their senses while inwardly fixed in drunkenness. "Each do We supply, both these and those, from the bounty of the Lord. And the bounty of thy Lord can never be limited."[7] The first duty upon him who is worthy and firm in vision is that he know God and His messengers by those attributes to which the verses of the Quran are signposts. Here he (ibn Ashir) informs us that this is the primary duty of one who is worthy, meaning mature. The meaning of maturity for the folk is that a man's gaze be firmly fixed upon God—that is, that he attain to the vision of the Truth so that the veil (of illusion) is lifted from him. This is the requirement for realization of God in all His manifestations. He who has not attained to a vision of the Truth, and thus has not had the veil lifted from him, is not worthy to know Him in the rest of His forms and attributes. These words are intended for one who is responsible, who has attained maturity and left the confinement of rules for the open space of unity (*al-tawḥīd*) and has realized God. This is the one who is held responsible for a task that no one beside him can accomplish. He it is who realizes God in all His attributes, and not merely in His Essence while denying His other manifestations, for he who is ignorant of the attributes is ignorant also of the One Attributed.

O brother, beware of having realized Him in Himself while denying Him in existence, for there is no outward other than Him. Beware of knowing Him in separation, or of knowing Him in reconciliation while being ignorant of Him in conflict. He wishes for you to know Him as He wills, and not as you will. Be with Him as one journeying with Him in His Essence, so that you do not deny Him in phenomena. He wishes that you know Him by experience and not merely by words. He teaches you and grants what you ask so that He remains within the realm of the Praised One. If you are ignorant, then ignorance is your abode. If you have knowledge, then He (*al-Ḥaqq*) is your Lord. Stop opposing Him and contemplate His beauty in all you see, for there is nothing other than Him, and say, as the author of *al-Insān al-Kāmil*[8] has said (may God be pleased with him!), "My Beloved's beauty is reflected within me, and in every gaze upon His face there arise overflowing yearnings." And another has said, "Look at My beauty which is witnessed by every man thus: there runs water under green shoots. Though all receive the same water, yet their flowers are varied in hue."[9]

The nature of God is oneness of Essence, attributes, and acts; for He is at the same time neither limited nor multiple. Thus he (Ibn Ashir) spoke of the oneness of Essence and attributes, lest one imagine, upon hearing of the timelessness of the attributes that these were separate eternal entities. Exalted is God above such things! To the oneness of God can be added nothing, for it does not permit any additions just as it permits no deficiency. "God was, and there was naught with Him. He is now even as he was." The attributes cannot stand alone to the degree that they become independent of His existence, nor can they be separate from that which they manifest, namely the Essence. This is the meaning of oneness of Essence and attributes. As for oneness of action, it means that there cannot possibly exist any act alongside the act of God, glorified and most high. Thus, one can say that men are divided into three groups: the first of these believes that there is no doer of actions save God, and they understand the oneness of action by means of its evidence and not by belief alone. They believe that the doer is one, even if the actions are multiple. These are the children of the path with regard to realization. The second group has realized the truth of the oneness of God's attributes. When a man has perceived this oneness, he sees only God in a being's hearing, seeing, living, speaking, power, willing, or knowing, and is heedful of the existence of the attributes in every creature by means of direct perception and not merely by proofs. For if we have realized that there is no doer save God, then we cannot associate these qualities with other than Him. The third group is those who have realized the truths of oneness of the Essence and preclude any created thing from this vision. When the greatness of His Essence is revealed to them, they can find therein no space for the existence of creatures, and thus they say there is nothing in reality save God, for they no longer possess anything other than Him. These are the people of the Essence (*al-dhātiyyūn*); these are the realized, the unifiers. Everyone else is veiled and negligent compared to them, for they have not partaken of the morsels of union, not breathed the air of uniqueness, but have only heard of this union, and where their hearing fails they believe that they have reached union. On the contrary! They are in fact distant and cut off from God, for union is not conveyed through writings, nor can it be explained by the eloquent in speech. Neither nations nor continents can contain it. So numerous are the secrets of the realized and those of the hearts of lovers, they cannot be borne even by the heavens and all their realms.

The Prophet (upon him be blessings and peace!) said, relating what was told to him by his Lord, "Neither my heavens nor my earth can contain Me, but the heart of my believing slave contains Me." O, what a heart and what a Master! What an abode and what a dweller therein! O God, dwell within our hearts, and take us not to task by Thy silence. When he (Ibn Ashir) had finished speaking of the Essence and the attributes that come from it, he began to explain the attributes upon which are laid the foundations of knowledge and through which forms contain realities and existence is adorned. The tongue proclaims the inner state of faith and security, for the Quran and the seven verses have been revealed.[10] A curtain has been spread over the manifestations of realities and the One veils Himself through attributes. On account of the power of the revelation of these attributes, they were veiled from men's eyes.

Then he (Ibn Ashir) said, (in speaking further of the attributes of God), "Power, will, knowledge, life, hearing, speech, sight, possessor of ordinances."

These attributes are veils that hide the Essence, for the power of God's manifestations necessitate their being covered and thus power is the veil of the Powerful; will is the veil of the One who Wills; knowledge is the veil of the Knower; life is the veil of the Living; hearing is the veil of the Hearer; sight is the veil of the Seer, and speech is the veil of the Speaker. Thus, the intelligible attributes are a veil upon the inner ones. He who stops at deeds has been veiled from beholding the attributes. He who stops at beholding the attributes is veiled from beholding the Essence. He who has known the Essence does not see anything other than it in all the secondary essences. He is the man who says, "The Essence is not veiled save by the Essence." The attributes are veiled from sight in the same way the Essence is veiled. Power is veiled through its irradiation, will is veiled by its own free inclinations (*khawāṭir*), speech is veiled by the diversity of its indications through letters and voices, and life is veiled by its association with the Essence. Hearing and sight are veiled by the intensity of their radiation into existence; knowledge is veiled by the power in which it encompasses and includes within it all known things. Then know that these attributes can be divided into three categories. To each category corresponds a world of reality. Hearing, sight, and speech belong to the terrestrial world (*ᶜālam al-nāsūt*). Power, will, and knowledge belong to the angelic world (*ᶜālam al-malakūt*). Life is from the archangelic domain (*ᶜālam al-jabarūt*). All of them are inseparable from the Essence, which encompasses them and transcends all things. To say that the attributes are attached to creation refers in Sufi terms to the idea that existence is bound by the archetypes, as reeds are woven in a mat. Existence is bound to its archetypes and not the other way around. The act and the One who acts are united before existence and remain thus in manifestation; a thing does not manifest of itself but is made to be manifest, for things in themselves are non-existent. Understand this!

In speaking of the attributes of the worshipper:

One of the attributes of the slave is weakness; power belongs only to God, the mighty and majestic. No one can share in it save Him, not even a great king or a prophet. All other than God is weak and has no power over the benefits or harm that befalls it save by God's will. "Verily those on whom ye call beside God will never create a fly, though they combine together for the purpose."[11] Of the attributes of the slave is also that of lack of will (*karāha*). As for the quality of will (*irāda*), it is of the qualities of the Living One, mighty and majestic. O slave, if you describe yourself with this quality, you have thereby described your Lord with the opposite quality, for you cannot both share in it, or covet its like. Know God by your own powers and you will fall from His pleasure. He who surrenders the power of willing to God lives in peace; and he who takes it from Him is condemned to the opposite; God, mighty and majestic says, "O my slave! You desire something and I desire something. If you submit to that which I desire, I will then fulfill what you desire, but if you contend with what I desire, I will try you with that which you desire, and there will be no will left except Mine." Leave, therefore, any willing to God, and choose not another act along with His. Will has been taken away from those realized in God, and questioning of what is divinely decreed is for the ignorant and heedless. In the first stage of the path the disciple has a desire and that is to devote himself to God. In the end he gives up his will to God. Thus willing is how he sets forth on the path and yet it is for that very thing that he is reproached. He who possesses a desire of his own when brought before God has strayed from the path of his Lord, so know, brother, that you are given the quality of lack of will, and conform to the attribute of God, namely His will. This is the will of which it has been said, "Submit to Selma, go where she goes, follow the traces of her resting-places, and turn to where she has turned."

Ignorance is another quality of the slave, for you are, O slave, ignorant of both yourself and your nature. How then could you ask to know God? You have the right to ask to know yourself and to realize your nature, and then you can turn to that which is outside of you. You do not know who you are, or where you came from. You merely found yourself manifested thus and began to awaken to this world, while fleeing from the other. The goal is knowledge of your soul that makes you say, "I am naught." You cannot know what this nothingness is, however, if you have imagined it to be a separate world whence you have come and where you will return. This would mean you have attributed some sort of existence to nothingness since you have made it a thing. The Prophet (peace and blessings be upon him!) said, "God was, and there was naught with Him."

There cannot be nothingness alongside of existence; if you put something permanent alongside His eternity, you have no knowledge nor any wisdom, but are ignorant, and even ignorant of your ignorance. Ask for someone to take you by the hand, and to awaken you to the presence of your Lord. Then your delusions will become transformed into understanding, and your ignorance into knowledge.

Another of the qualities of the slave is death. Life is not an attribute of yours such that it could be said to belong to you, for you are but a dead man with the form of one alive. An example for you is a crazy man in whom there lives a *jinn* who says, "I am so-and-so," when in fact he is not. If you fling yourself before your Lord, throwing before him your body as your forefather Adam did (peace be upon him!) then He will breathe into you of His spirit, forgive you and create you according to His creation. Then you may truly say, "I am alive." God, mighty and majestic, said: "He hath created man from a drop of fluid, yet behold! He is an open opponent."[12] Therefore, return, brother, to your attribute of death, keep firmly to your place, and do not desire what is not yours, so that God might strengthen you by His spirit.

Another quality of the slave is deafness; you are now, O slave, deaf. The ability to hear is not one of your qualities, for God alone is the hearer. Whenever you attribute the ability to hear to yourself, you become deaf. Although the quality of hearing is there, you cannot hear, for if you could, you would surely hear the speech of God at every moment and in every circumstance, for the Glorified has never ceased to speak. It is impossible according to His nature for Him to be silent. Where is your ability to hear His words? And where is your understanding of them? You are deaf and remain within the folds of non-existence. If you entered true existence you would surely hear the speech of the Worshipped One. But how can a deaf man hear a call to him? If you heard you would answer, but how could you answer when you are marked by dumbness? If you are dumb, how then can you speak, when that is of the attributes of your Lord? If you could speak, you would surely be suitable to be taught, but the dumb man cannot sit with such men. Thus you are prevented from attaining the station of those who converse and have discourse. If you truly realized your dumbness, He would extend to you of His words and you would speak with His tongue and have discourse with Him, until your hearing became one with His, and you were to hear nothing save what comes from Him.

Another of your qualities, O slave, is blindness. You are blind, for if you had eyes, you would surely see Him according to His name the Outwardly Manifest (*al-Ẓāhir*). Now you see only phenomena, but where is the manifestation of God, who is the most evident of all manifestations in the visible world? Exalted be God above having any veil over His appearance. It is but your own quality of blindness that has overcome you. You have become blind while still seeing and attributing the latter to your own power. If you indeed realized your attribute and approached your Lord according to His pleasure, He would surely become your hearing and your sight, and when that happened, you would no longer hear anything but Him, nor see anything but Him, for you would be hearing with His ears, and seeing with His eyes. This is the goal attained by drawing near to God and devoting yourself to Him. So declare, brother, your quality of blindness and ponder the wisdom therein; glimmers of sight will appear to you, and you will then hear what you did not hear before and see what you did not see before. This will not come true for you save by knowing yourself and contemplating that which is non-existent in your nature.

The truth of the Essence has no truth lacking in it, and for this reason I have called it the Truth of truths. Nothing can exist without possessing an underlying truth in the creation. The preceding derives from His words, "Wheresoever ye turn, there is the Face of God."[13] If opposition did not exist, contrast could not be manifested, and no one can understand this save one who has realized unity of the Essence of God and all that belongs to it. The one veiled from God may think that by "unity" it is meant that God is One in the sense that His Essence has nothing else combined in it, or that there exists no other essence which can be likened unto it; he does not realize that the oneness of God cannot admit of anything sharing existence within it. When did something exist that could be compared to it? The Quran has said: "There is naught like unto Him." This is so on account of the non-existence of things. This world does not count as a thing, but as non-thing. At the same time, do not believe that it is other than, or foreign to, the divine Presence; it is but an irradiation from it, a secret from among Its Secrets, a light from among its Lights. God has said: "God is the Light of the heavens and the earth."[14] "Thus did we show Abraham the kingdom of the heavens and the earth."[15] When he saw a star he said, "This is my Lord." But he did not utter this as if to liken something to God—he was protected from that—and He has told us of how He revealed to him His kingdom; rather, Abraham said it as one who has perfectly understood the transcendence of God, and as one shown the Truth of truths, as the noble verse indicates, "Wheresoever ye turn, there is the Face of God."[16] He declared this truth to his people, that they might learn to worship God in everything, for this is the highest point of piety, "Fear God with true piety." When they were unable to understand this subtle truth, their fault became evidence against them and this is what is meant by the verse, "This is Our argument. We gave it unto Abraham against his folk. We raise unto degrees of wisdom whom We will."[17] When the kingdoms of the heavens and the earth were revealed to him, he realized that the reality of the One who makes things to exist was present in every existing thing, and he wanted to speak of this knowledge he had realized, but he found their hearts turned away from the pure unity of God, that unity which He alone possesses. When Abraham saw them in this state he said, "O my people! Verily I am innocent of what you associate with God. Verily I have turned my face to Him who created the heavens and the earth, as one by nature upright, and I am not of the idolaters."[18] God is the Guide who leads us to the straight path.

Some gnostics have said that the prophets lie at the feet of the saints. The truth is that the gnostic has a time, as the Prophet (peace and blessings be upon him!) said, "I have a time in which nothing suffices me save my Lord." At that time, extinction in God overcomes the gnostic, who is drowned and annihilated in Him to the point where he leaves his senses and his identity, leaving behind all his perceptions and his existence. This is his annihilation in the Essence of God, the glorified and most high; the divine Holiness then descends upon him in such abundance that he bears witness to his essence as one with God's Essence on account of his realization and his annihilation. He declares his state in this realm by saying, "Glory be to me! There is no god but me alone," and by saying, "Majestic is my might, and holy my greatness." He is forgiven this, for the faculty with which he perceives things and meanings, and by which he discerns for each their level according to the knowledge of their qualities, is no longer his; it has been obliterated, done away with, annihilated. Upon the loss and disappearance of this faculty and the simultaneous abundance of the holy secret in him, he begins to speak with words whose author is God; he is given to be His representative and speaks with the tongue of God, not with his own, and expresses things according to God's Essence, not according to his own. It is from this realm that we have the words of Abu Yazid al-Bistami (may God be pleased with him!): "Glory be to me! How magnificent am I!" And the words of al-Hallaj, "I am God (*Ana al-Ḥaqq*), whose Essence changes not. Time may pass but there exists naught but God in these clothes." Another one said, "The earth is mine, the heavens are mine." And as in the words of al-Shushtari (may God be pleased with him!):

> I appear as something extraordinary
> To whoever has seen me.
> I am the lover, I am the Beloved
> There is no other.

Ibn al-Farid has said many similar things. These words are spoken in a state of extinction in God (*al-fanāʾ*) proportioned to their station and dignity. Such souls are exalted to a degree equal to that of the prophets. Understand, brother, that these masters' words were uttered while in a state of absorption and extinction in the majesty of God and outside of themselves, and do not therefore be deceived into thinking this way yourself, as long as you are of sound mind; even if you have attained the furthest reaches of realization, you are not permitted to compare yourself to a prophet, for you are conscious and of sound mind. It is of the first importance to know that intelligence is one of the conditions of responsibility and he who takes such responsibility opposes any departure from correct behavior, unlike he who is overwhelmed by a state and utters words such as those mentioned earlier. The latter is not blamed for his actions, but if he were of sound mind he could not say such things, for every gnostic knows that he is far from the degree of prophecy. He sees his incapacity in every matter, unlike the prophets, for they have been created with perfect submission and infallibility. If the saints are given divine protection (*ḥifẓ*), this protection cannot be taken away; moreover it comes only with sanctity and not before it, unlike leadership which exists before prophethood and after it. This is why you see such qualities in them and in no one else.

It was mentioned in the beginning of this work that for the gnostics one word may comprise several meanings; the author (Ibn Ashir) did not mention this explicitly in his work but only alluded to it briefly, fearing lest the reader misunderstand him. He went on to explain and clarify the phrase, "There is no divinity but God, Muhammad is the Messenger of God," saying that these words encompass every possible meaning, and by this statement he means everything inward, outward, invisible, and visible. Or, one could say as well, everything sensed, perceived, unknown, and known, or again, everything existing and non-existing. To say "there is no divinity save God" is to say, "and God encompasses all things"[19] without end. "Say: Though the sea became ink for the words of my Lord, verily the sea would be used up before the words of my Lord were exhausted, even though We brought the like thereof to help."[20] If you realize that "there is no divinity save God" encompasses all meanings and that everything is included in it, you must then conclude that there exists nothing but the truth that "there is no divinity save God" or say, with one enlightened, "all who seek the Beloved, He is present in creation itself." Shaykh al-Harraq said,

> In your beauty is gathered all desires.
> For us there is naught but Your Countenance.
> All else vanishes from my sight
> When the beauty of Your Countenance appears to me.

The sage is not truly realized until he knows God in all His aspects. He must master each one and preserve none but that of the Essence of God. "Wheresoever ye turn, there is the Face of God," meaning wheresoever you turn your senses in the sensory world, or your mind in the world of the known, or your imaginings in the world of intuitions, there is the Face of God. In every "where" (*ayn*), there is an essence (*ᶜayn*). All is "there is no divinity save God," and that is why he (the author) said it encompasses every meaning. He is the first and the last and if you have understood this, then you will also realize His beauty, majesty, and the combination of both of these attributes in His perfection, which is one with the divine Essence, majestic and glorious. This is the meaning of the participation of existence in the testimony of unity (*shahāda*). You must also include within this the name of the noblest of slaves, and this is found in the words "Muhammad is the Messenger of God." The words in this noble utterance are on the same level as those of Jesus (peace be upon him!) speaking in the name of the Father, the Mother, and the Son. These words comprise both the Muhammadan message and the divine message. From this one can see that the words "Muhammad is the Messenger of God" contain within them the three worlds: the creation (*al-mulk*), the angelic domain (*al-malakūt*), and the archangelic domain (*al-jabarūt*). The word "Muhammad" refers to the earthly domain; it is the sensorial manifestation of creatures. The word "Messenger" refers to the angelic world; namely the secrets within existence; it is a link between the temporal and the eternal, and it is also called the "Guardian Spirit." The word "God" refers to the archangelic domain; this is the ocean from which archetypal ideas and symbols pour forth. We spoke of the word "Messenger" saying that it was the link between the temporal and the eternal. Yes, he is the intermediary, since if it were not for him, the world would perish. If the temporal came face to face with the eternal, the former would cease to exist and only the eternal would remain. When the Messenger represented the two domains, the world became well-ordered, for outwardly he is a drop of clay, but inwardly he is the representative of the Lord of the worlds. Know further that the Messenger is symbolized by the word *barzakh* (isthmus) mentioned in the verse, "He hath loosed the two seas. They meet. There is a barrier (*barzakh*) between them, and they encroach not one upon the other."[21] If it were not for the *barzakh* of the Messenger, the world would become inverted and the worshipper would become the worshipped, for if you take away the word "Messenger" from "Muhammad is the Messenger of God" the meaning becomes "Muhammad is God" and this is impossible.

The pillars of Islam are five, the two Testimonies
being the bases for all the rest.

Ibn Ashir is telling us here (may God have mercy on him!) that the one practicing this way cannot be firmly established in it save by means of the pillars, which are five in number. If he neglects one of them, his order will perish and he will observe his own destruction and annihilation. He then said that the two Testimonies are the conditions for the rest of the rules or pillars. The inward characteristic of the Prophet (peace and blessing be upon him!) is the consciousness of the divine (*al-mushāhada al-uluhiyya*) and pious works, "and we sent thee not save as a mercy to the worlds."[22] He who enters into these two stations has attained the highest possible rank, for he is strong in both aspects. The one who witnesses but one aspect is like he who has attained the station of extinction in the Divine and remains in that state without comprehending the aspect of the "message" and what it demands of slavehood. He is therefore deficient in relation to others. In the same way, he who has comprehended and borne witness to the Muhammadan presence without realizing the truths of slavehood and gaining knowledge which will free him from the need for indirect proofs and indications, can experience no direct witnessing or contemplation, and is thus deficient, and unable to be counted among the realized. One must keep firmly to both (Testimonies) as the author has said: "These two Testimonies are the bases for all the rest." These bases or conditions demand of their existence your inexistence. If the gnostic bore witness to neither of these two first things, then upon what could he base himself? Thus, He made the rest of the rules easy to aid in the establishment of the first two.

And then prayer, almsgiving of portion, and fasting
and pilgrimage for whosoever is able.

The second pillar is prayer; its link with the testimony of faith (*shahāda*) aids in bringing about the latter, for the gnostic can only prostrate himself after having borne witness to the One worshipped; the word prayer (*ṣalāt*) is derived from the root *ṣila* (bonding, uniting), and means entering into the state of worship such that the gnostic be joined (*mawṣūl*) and not parted (*mafṣūl*) from God. Prayer (*al-ṣalāt*) refers to the prayer of union, not that of separation. This prayer is obligatory in the world of the spirit, not in that of forms. We will speak further about this in the section devoted to it. The third pillar is almsgiving (*zakāt*), and it means that the slave should spend of all that God has blessed him to possess, and all that was created for His sake. Everything has its form of almsgiving; the almsgiving of the gnostic is to give himself and his possessions to his Lord. We will speak more of this also in the appropriate section, and about what is required and what is not for *zakāt*. The fourth pillar is the fast. Fasting means to withdraw from a thing. And fasting among the Sufis means to withdraw from all other than God; we will explain this in its section, God willing. The fifth pillar is the pilgrimage. It means to make a pilgrimage to the Lord of the house and to make the circumambulation (*ṭawāf*) of the heart in the beatific presence of the Beloved. The words "for whosoever is able" refers to the subtleties of union, to the complete annihilation of the pilgrim such that he no longer possesses anything of himself. We will speak of this later.

A gnostic asked me about the meaning of the word "descent" (*nuzūl*) in the Quran, and I answered him according to his state, saying, "Brother, the words of God come neither by letters nor by voice, as you think, for He is the most high and exalted of all things. He has descended to the point where His Reality became manifested as letters and voices. This is the meaning of the 'descent' (*nuzūl*)." These words were sweeter to him than honey, for he is required to have faith in all the messengers (upon them be blessings and peace!). He used to say, in a state of spiritual drunkenness, "*Allāh, Allāh*" or to say as Aisha[23] said, (may God be pleased with her!) when she was told, "Give thanks to God and to His Messenger." She replied, "I will give thanks only to God." If his senses took hold of him again he might say, "I have been given what the messengers have not," or as Abd al-Qadir al-Jilani said, (may God be pleased with him!): "O prophets, you have brought a name (*laqab*) and we have brought what you did not." This manner of expression springs from their states and the one who speaks thus should return to his proper level until he sees his station in relation to the station of the prophets like that of a youth before his parents. The Messengers (peace and blessings be upon them!) enjoy a relationship with God that the saint cannot attain. Whenever we observe their state and see in them a lack of strength, that is a sign of our failure to grasp their station. Even the apparent disobedience of a prophet, as it is depicted in the Book, does not depart from obedience, although we cannot understand it with our minds. For this reason they must be held above all deficiencies whatsoever. A brother of ours was once speaking with me, for he had some doubt concerning the matter of the prophet Jacob and his grief for Joseph (peace be upon them both!), as it is told in the story: "And his eyes were whitened with the sorrow he was suppressing."[24] The brother asked, "How could he grieve so much, and esteem the beauty of Joseph above that of God?" He referred as an argument to the lines by Ibn al-Farid (may God be pleased with him!): "If they had made mention of His face to Jacob, the beauty of Joseph's face would have been forgotten." I humored him until he had come out of the state he was in, and then I explained to him that Jacob did not grieve for the sake of Joseph in himself, but insofar as he was a manifestation of the exalted and blessed Divinity. In the presence of Joseph he felt the Divine closer to him, and he became the vehicle of God's manifestation to Jacob. He was also manifest to Moses on Mount Sinai, and he did not feel such great proximity with God except on this mount in spite of the fact that He is everywhere present, "He is with you wheresoever ye may be."[25] In the same way, the prophet Jacob perceived the beauty of God in the form of Joseph and it became unbearable to be separated from him, for he had become his *qibla* (orientation in prayer). In this regard the Prophet (peace and blessing be upon him!) said, "I saw my Lord in the form of a beardless youth." There is no doubt that when he saw God, blessed and exalted, in this youth, he did not permit him to leave him. This is also the meaning of the angels' prostration to Adam (peace be upon him!), for God blessed and exalted, created him in His image, and from this again we see the prostration by some of the Christians before Jesus during his life and their description of him as divine. Everyone mentioned above was prostrating themselves to God, and to no other, for His beauty is so strongly manifest in certain forms that what is left of the human becomes annihilated in His existence. Those who have perfected their intellects, such as the prophets and the chosen saints, see the One who manifests in the form, not the form by itself. Their realization is of God's transcendence, not of any limitation or analogy. When they bear witness to a form among others their witnessing is joined to His name the "Outwardly Manifest" (*al-Ẓāhir*) and differs from the limited view of the Christians, and those of their way, because each time God appeared to them in a form they stopped short at it and were veiled from the ultimate manifestation. He then caused them to go astray in their knowledge. This refers back to the grief that the prophet Jacob felt for Joseph; he drew nearer to God upon seeing his son and when he lost him his perception of God left him and for this reason he was saddened, but he did not lose sight of the Spirit of God, and thus he said to his sons: "Go, my sons, and ascertain concerning Joseph and his brother, and despair not of the Spirit of God."[26] Joseph was for him identical with the Spirit of God. When my questioner had understood these explanations he said, "In that case, he was correct to grieve, and if I had understood the nature of Joseph, I would have grieved along with him."

Faith (*īmān*) requires the existence of the scales on the Day of Judgment, and requires that one's deeds be weighed upon them in the manner in which God decrees. The gnostic, in the state of total absorption in God, oblivious of the existence of creatures and of their deeds even when he returns to his senses within existence, may say, "And God hath created you and that which you do."[27] How can a work be weighed when He is the doer of it? Through constant striving, one can understand the meaning of works and how they are related to God by means of a subtle link. The deeds of the gnostics are weighed at the moment of their death, but God, blessed and most high, finds no works accumulated with them on account of their absorption in the Doer and their inattention to the deeds. God, powerful and majestic, says to them, "Where are your deeds?" and they reply, "Where is our existence?" He says, "By what have you striven for Me?" and they reply, "By Yourself have we striven for You, by Yourself have we known You." He accepts them because of this—indeed, how would He not, when they abstained from everything by virtue of what they knew of Him, and left aside existence for the sake of contemplating Him. May God not forbid us what they have been given! You know already that the gnostics have a death before the physical death, as the Prophet (peace and blessings be upon him!)

has shown: "Die before ye die." This first death is the true one; anything else is but a journey. The true nature of death among the Sufis is the extinction, annihilation, and naughting of the slave. The gnostic may be dead to his ego and to the world in his essence, and be transported to his Lord, so that were you to ask him concerning himself he would not answer you, for he does not perceive his individuality or his ego. Abu Yazid al-Bistami (may God be pleased with him!) was asked concerning himself and he replied, "Abu Yazid is dead, may God not have mercy on him." This is truly death. As for the general death, if you were to ask one who died thus who he was on the Last Day, he would reply, "I am so-and-so." Such as he is still living, he has not yet breathed the fragrance of death, but has only journeyed from one world to another. No one can understand the nature of this death save he who has died, and such people are those who meet God before the general judgment. The Prophet (peace and blessings be upon him!) said: "Take account of yourselves before ye are taken to account." Strive, therefore and take yourselves to account until you are left free to contemplate your Lord.

Concerning *iḥsān*,[28] he who knows has said, "It is that you worship God as if thou sawest Him. And if thou seest Him not, yet verily He seeth thee." Religion is comprised of three levels, so cleave to the highest for your protection. If you wish to know the station of *iḥsān*, listen to him who has known and realized it (upon him be blessings and peace!) and who said that it is to "worship God as if thou sawest Him." This is the first stage of *iḥsān* and is here expressed as a state of watchfulness. The final stage of *iḥsān*, the attainment of direct contemplation and experience, begins with certitude and ends with direct vision. The path towards this station is taken up by the slave, but its perfection is granted by God. He, mighty and exalted, speaks of this: "If my slave draws near to Me by a hand's length, I will draw near to him by an arm's length; if he comes to Me walking, I will go to him running."[29] Thus, the beginning of the journey is made by the slave through the mercy of God. The one desirous of attaining this state must excel in vigilance and watchfulness of God secretly and openly, in seclusion and in the world, until the existence of all else is effaced from his consciousness. When God sees the sincerity of his worship He will appear to him, mighty and exalted, for He is not distant from His slave. The Prophet (peace and blessings be upon him!) said, "Be watchful of God, ye will find Him before ye." Therefore be watchful, O disciple, in your worship and in all your other circumstances as if you saw your Lord, and adhere to correct behavior, conscious that you are with Him, for you are not veiled from God by the existence of things with Him, but rather, you are veiled by your lack of watchfulness of His ordinances, as is mentioned by Ibn Ata Allah (may God be pleased with him!), "All that veils you from direct witnessing of Him is your failure to heed His ordinances." Therefore heed, O disciple, the ordinances of God and do not heed your own existence and ascribe works to yourself; rather, seek the help of God in His worship. Whenever you ascribe a thing to yourself you are thereby cut off from God. Would that you efface yourself for the existence of God; if you do not, how will you find your Lord, when you are only looking at yourself? This is shown in the Sufis' words (may God be pleased with them!): "If you are present, God will be absent, and if you are absent, your Lord will be present," and it is told by tradition that Moses (peace be upon him!) said to God, mighty and majestic, "How can I be united to you, O Lord of the worlds?" and He answered,

"Leave aside yourself and come." Therefore depart, brother, from yourself, your existence, and the frame of your body and rise up to your Lord; you will surely find Him nearer to you than your own existence. As long as you existed along with Him, you did not see Him; when you ceased to exist along with Him you saw Him. The author (may God be pleased with him!) said, "By that by which you do not see Him," meaning if you do not exist along with Him you will see Him. If you say, "How will I see Him when I do not exist with Him?" I would say, "You will see Him by His eyes, not by yours, for you are situated in time and the temporal cannot perceive the eternal. When your sight becomes His you will see Him." It is related that He said, "My slave ceases not to draw near to Me with voluntary acts of worship until I love him, and when I love him I become his hearing and his sight."[30] When this sight becomes that of God—and by sight here is meant the vision of the intellect (*al-baṣīra*)—he sees Him by it, that is, he sees God by His Self, not by his self, for when the temporal joins with the eternal the temporal perishes and the eternal remains.

Thus we can say that only God sees God: "Vision comprehendeth Him not, while He comprehendeth all vision."[31] How could it comprehend Him when He is closer to it than itself? Does the eye see itself, or does it rather see what is other than it? If you wish, brother, to know the One who exists, participate not in His projected existence. Descend the degree of existence to the lowest rung of non-existence. If you achieve this, knowledge of God will come to you, and you will be in His presence and unconscious of all other than He. Then you will live a life without death, and will know happiness without rupture. Be not content, brother, with less than this station, or suffice yourself with anything other than this goal, and say, "*Islam* is our sufficiency," for your *islam* is not perfected before the attainment of this station, as the author (may God be pleased with him!) says, "Religion is composed of three things, so grasp them with your firmest grasp," meaning that religion is comprised of these three parts and whoever takes hold of them has taken the firmest hold. Therefore arise, brother, and seek this noble station, for it is the end goal of what precedes it, that is, the end goal of *islam* and the end goal of *īmān* (faith), and this is why it is called *iḥsān*, or the perfection and knowledge of a thing. He who has no portion of the station of *iḥsān* is deficient in his *islam* in relation to others. *Iḥsān* comes from the root *aḥsana* and this signifies attainment to the highest degrees of religion and emulation of the Prophet which cannot be surpassed. One of this station bears three responsibilities: one for his body, one for his spirit, and one for his secret (essence). Each of these has a portion allotted to it. That of the body is *islam* and its duties, that of the spirit is *īmān* and its creed, and that of the secret is *iḥsān* and its realizations. And he (the author) said (may God be pleased with him!),

The divisions of the law are five: the obligatory, the recommended, the disliked, the forbidden, and the allowable. The commanded is either obligatory or recommended.

The divisions of law among the Sufis are five, meaning that they can be no more than these: the first category is the obligatory, and it is the realization of the One that is obligatory. Realization among the Sufis is their primary obligation, and the realized man is also known as he who is "unique," according to his words (peace and blessings be upon him!): "Verily God is One and He loves those who are one." Contemplation of this is the end goal. The second division is that of the recommended, and this is an allusion to the pleasing, desirable, and beloved, which refers to the chosen and beloved one (*al-muṣṭafa*) (upon him be blessings and peace!). The one who acts as he does, who follows in his footsteps, and who takes on his qualities is also to be called beloved and desired, for the follower is as a part of the one followed. The third category is the strongly discouraged. This means, among the Sufis, forgetfulness and preoccupation with things outside of these two noble stations, following a state of realization, which however are not excessive enough to become forbidden. This fourth category, the forbidden, is the vision of that which is outside God, as was mentioned. One who behaves in this way is in a state of sin, at the farthest degree of disobedience, and one fears his abandonment by God. The fifth division of the law is the allowable. It is permitted, among the Sufis, that one of them act towards people in such a way that he causes them to be kinder to one another while keeping watch over his heart (*sirr*) at all times lest these works lead him to forgetfulness and he enter the realm of the disliked and perhaps even that of the forbidden, and his heart become veiled from the vision of his Lord. Surely the gnostic must stand guard at the door of the heart and not be veiled by falling outside of His oneness. When he (Ibn Ashir) had finished speaking of the legal divisions of the law, he distinguished within the realm of the obligatory, saying,

The obligatory is divided into two categories: the accidental and the essential. The accidental category includes the Sunna as well.

Here he states that the realization of God is obligatory for the Sufis, and is divided into two categories: striving towards a realization that is an essential obligation of every individual, and the attainment of that which is known as total realization, that of the heart; it is manifest by the heart's eye seeing through illusion by certainty, by direct contemplation, and by vision. The one who has realized this state cannot explain it; he has attained a pure, unmixed knowledge by which he can aid his soul, but he is unable to aid others by it. This type of realization is an obligation upon every individual. The other type of realization is the secondary or accidental type; it brings eminence to he who has attained it, and gives him an understanding of the path and the means of travel upon it to God, mighty and majestic, for it consists of discernment and knowledge of the hidden depths of the soul and how to treat it, of the different types of realization, and of the ability to explain stations, states, and degrees. When a man is given this knowledge and sets out to help others by it, it is thereby removed from others, for it is not possible that everyone advance to the position of master; there are those who pass into obscurity and those who become known. Know further that this division also includes the *Sunna*, for there is an essential *Sunna* and a secondary *Sunna*. An example of the essential *Sunna* among the Sufis is an understanding (discernment) of that which the gnostic must accomplish in his religion, and an example of the secondary *Sunna* is knowledge of that by which the gnostic can enrich his disciples above others. Whether he be among men or occupied with his soul, the essential *Sunna* is sufficient and all should strive to empty the heart so that it can witness its Lord.

The book of prayer

Prayer is the noblest way to draw near to God and occupies the highest of degrees, for it is derived from the word *ṣila* (link), that which joins together. There can be no doubt that prayer is the link that joins the servant to his Lord, therefore one speaks of arrival (*al-wuṣūl*). When the servant arrives to his Lord he has attained the prayer of union (*al-ittiṣāl*) that can never thereafter be broken, as one (may God have mercy on him!) said, "After their arrival there was no return. After they prostrated themselves, they did not rise up again." It is of this that the Prophet (peace and blessings be upon him!) said: "My eyes are refreshed by prayer." This prayer, which refreshes the eyes of the Prophet, is the final goal of the gnostics. He who has been given of this prayer has been given all. The petitions of the gnostics, the mutterings of those in ecstasy, and the disciple's desire for this station goes on increasing until the book (of prayer) achieves its purpose, for those who know God are those who have been given this prayer. As for the rest, they have no knowledge of it—nay, they cannot even imagine it on account of their lack of realization.

He who is ignorant of something becomes its enemy. A group of religious scholars went to a gnostic in Egypt with the purpose of disputing with him. The gnostic said to them, "Is there among you scholars a man who prays?" They were pleased by these words, and replied, "Is there anyone among us who has missed a prayer?" (of the five canonical prayers). He then said, "You are those whom God has set apart from the rest by His words, 'Man was created anxious; fretful when evil toucheth him, and when good toucheth him, grudging; save those who pray.'"[32] They fell silent, for they did not understand this type of prayer, granted to those whom God favors and by which He guides whoever strives toward Him. For this reason the Prophet (peace and blessings be upon him!) said, "My eyes are refreshed by prayer." It is the abode of nearness to God and the fulfillment of all desire; outwardly it is prayer, but inwardly it is union. It is the bond that joins the worshipper and Worshipped. Outwardly worship, it is inwardly utter absorption (in Him).

On the obligations of prayer:

Among the obligations of prayer is the prostration. As the summit of the act of worship, it is an expression of the servant's lowering of himself to the utmost point of non-existence. This lowering is known among the Sufis as the extinction (*fanāʾ*) of the self in the Self. It is in the state of prostration that the worshipper draws nearest to his Lord, and of the one in this state God, mighty and majestic, has said, "Prostrate thyself and draw near."[33]

The author (Ibn Ashir) said, "The conditions (for prayer) are to face the *qibla*, to be cleansed of filth, to cover the private parts, and to purify oneself." He tells us that the conditions for attaining to God, mighty and majestic, are four: the first of these is to face the *qibla*. By this he means that the traveler on the path must dedicate his heart to abiding in the presence of God, mighty and majestic. This condition applies from the beginning of the path, for whosoever desires union must devote himself exclusively to the *Kaᶜaba* which represents the divine Presence. The traveler can only devote his soul to the essence of this *Kaᶜaba* by contemplating it with the "eye of certainty" (*ᶜayn al-yaqīn*) or the "realization of certainty" (*ḥaqq al-yaqīn*). If he possesses only "the lore of certainty" (*ᶜilm al-yaqīn*) he cannot see the essence of the *qibla*, for he is still behind the veil and is at a great distance from God, mighty and majestic. He must devote himself with vigilance until, when he turns slightly away from the *qibla,* no harm befalls him. He who strives to pierce the veil is not harmed by slight distractions. An example of this is given by the one who strives in the path of God, mighty and majestic, but whose striving contains a distraction, namely his asking for union, which has caused his worship to be performed for this purpose. It is more correct for him to devote his worship to God and not to some goal or other. Nevertheless this goal does no harm to beginners and that is why it is called a light distraction. It comes from one veiled from God; if it come from a position of proximity to the spiritual *Ka^caba*, as would be the case if one possessed the realization of certainty, it would be called a great distraction—indeed, it would cause a removal from the *Ka^caba*. Now, if I said that acts for the purpose of union with God are a distraction, what should I say of acts performed to obtain a reward? I would say this has no part in the seeking of God or in the path to Him. The one in this state is not counted among the travelers to God, for he is not on the path to Him, but on the path to heaven, and the end of his travels to it, that is to heaven, will not be to the Lord of heaven. The Prophet (peace and blessings be upon him!) said, "Whoever emigrates for God and His Messenger, his emigration is for God and His Messenger, and whoever emigrates for a worldly aim or to marry a woman, his emigration is for that for which he sets out." And know that this *qibla* in which there appears a distraction exists only for travelers on the path and those who keep watch over their goal. As for those who are united and firm in their vision, it is not possible for them to turn aside from the *qibla*, for it entirely surrounds them, and they are drowned in it to the point that if one of them attempted to look away from it he could not—how can one turn away from a *qibla* when he is within it? And if one who is in the physical *Ka^caba* cannot turn away from it, how then can he who is in the spiritual *Ka^caba* which is identical with the divine Presence?

The second condition for lawful prayer is the removal of filth. This condition is required before and throughout its execution. The one facing God, mighty and majestic, in prayer must have his place, his garments, and his body completely pure of filth, and by "filth" is meant the existence of disobedience, wherever it may be found. Purification of place alludes to the outward, and purification of garments, to the inward, that is, to the heart. Purification of the body is an allusion to the purification of the most inward of the inward, namely the secret (*sirr*). The outward cannot be purified save by keeping to the law, performing what is ordered, and avoiding what is forbidden. The inner man, that is, the heart, cannot be purified save by keeping to the path and leaving aside all vices such as envy, hatred, pride, desire, and vanity, and from everything that is contrary to purity. Purification of the secret means total purification for God, mighty and majestic. The mightiest of speakers said, "And thy garment purify";[34] if the purification of the garment, which is an allusion to the heart, is demanded, what then of the purification of the Heart of hearts, the abode of the Lord? One at this station must stop short at the door of his heart. Whenever anything other than God occurs to him he must silence it with the force of the Absolute One. He who desires entrance into the presence of God, mighty and majestic, must be pure of soul, facing his Lord, and paying no attention to distractions away from his *qibla* not acquiring any impurity, for these two conditions hold for the beginning and throughout. He must not devote himself at the beginning and turn away at the end, or purify himself at the beginning and dirty himself at the end. He must, rather, remain on the way of his heart, devoted to his Lord, wary of the dirt and impurities of the world, and whenever he is afflicted by its evils he must purify himself of them immediately, according to His words: "Verily God loveth those who turn in repentance, and loveth those who purify themselves."[35]

The third condition for true prayer is the covering of the private parts, and by this is meant the covering of all that it is necessary to conceal in the path. The one who wishes union with God, whose secret Essence is hidden, must conceal the lights that appear to him, for the secret Essence of God demands reverence, and to revere it is to conceal it from the outside. It was said, "Gratitude for secrets means preserving them from phenomena." If the divine Secret is not kept concealed but is shown on earth and if one speaks of what should remain unsaid, the private parts are uncovered. One has said, "whoever speaks of the secret Essence of God, God makes him speak of his shameful acts." He cuts him off from His presence for his failure to observe the pact with God, which, made in His presence, excludes all who are foreign to it. Whosoever makes light of God's secret will most certainly fall from the Essence on account of his failure to guard it and his treachery. His link will be severed, and he shall return from whence he knew not. "And thy Lord is not at all a tyrant to His slaves."[36] It is said in this regard, "Were men of knowledge to preserve it, they would be preserved. Were they to venerate it in their hearts, they would be venerated. But they trifled with it and dirtied its goodness by their passion until it was destroyed." Know further that this condition of concealment is obligatory alongside mindfulness. As for the one of this station who is overwhelmed by it, that is, one lacking any ability to conceal it, he does not thereby have his prayer violated or become cut off from his path. He is excused, for his intelligence by which he discerns between things and by which he differentiates various levels and stations has left him, and with the removal of his discernment his responsibility is also removed, as the author has mentioned before. Responsibility is conditional upon presence of mind, and there is no blame upon him who has lost the latter, as one has said, "So do not blame the drunkard in his state of inebriation, for in our drunkenness responsibility is waived and we are made free of it." He who is overcome by his state is not subject to the condition of concealment, as the author (may God be pleased with him!) said:

In mindfulness and ability, except the last,
and there are many incapable.

This means that each of the conditions assume mindfulness and ability, save the last, which is cleansing from a state of legal impurity. This condition is not part of being mindful or able, but is rather a duty from the start to the finish. By impurity (*ḥadath*) is meant the created order (*ḥudūth*), which encompasses all that is apart from God. He who wishes union with God must rid himself of this great impurity which veils him from Him. Whosoever stops at this veil is cut off from his Lord, and there can be no entrance to Him save by lifting it. In the introduction to this book the means of ridding oneself of impurity were explained. Let the disciple know that the removal of impurity is a condition which goes hand in hand with the existence of mindfulness and ability as well as with the existence of negligence and weakness.

Whoever enters the presence of the Eternal purified of existence (*ḥudūth*), stripped of the dualities of the lower world, and then becomes distracted by existence, is judged to have broken his state of purity and must renew it each time he is afflicted thus. Let him not deal lightly with that which has kept him from abiding with God, mighty and majestic, until He no longer looks towards the heart which used to abide with Him. How could He look at a heart that carries the image of something other than Him upon it? The Mighty and Majestic does not accept idolatrous acts, so how could He accept an idolatrous heart? Beware! Do not mingle temporal existence with the Eternal. The author[37] of the *Ḥikam* has said, "How can a heart be illumined that carries the images of creatures upon its mirror?" To endeavor to combine these two poles is impossible. It is like combining motion with stillness, for the darkness of created things is contrary to the lights of realization. O you who lay claim to realization! Where is your vision of the One? You have fallen among His creation. O you who lay claim to knowledge of the divine realm! How often have you been purified and lost your purity, and how often have you taken an oath and broken it? You have made a pact with God not to regard anything other than Him, so how is it you have turned your gaze to the created world? O you who claim to be in awe of God, do you not pay heed to the one who said, "How can existence appear out of naught?" or he who said, "How can the temporal abide with He who possesses the attribute of eternity?"

In conclusion, the presence of God, mighty and majestic, is exalted above all else. Therefore he who is tempted while in this realm must pay heed, remind himself, cleanse and purify himself according to the words of the Most High: "Verily, those who ward off evil, when a glamour from the devil troubleth them, they do but remember God, and behold them seers."[38] Each time one is afflicted with impurity he is removed from the presence of God, and there is no difference between one who consciously intends it or otherwise.

They, that is, the Sufis (may God be pleased with them!) have said: "Realization of the end is the return to the origin." Neither he who is weak nor he who is overcome and reveals what should remain concealed is prevented from this "return," for he who is weak enters by permission and God accepts him in this state. He must not work corruption in the earth after his righteousness, but must rather strive in the purpose for which he entered God's presence. They, that is, the Sufis (may God be pleased with them!) have said, "We will not leave aside something by which we enter God's presence," and it is said that Bishr al Hafi (may God be pleased with him!) lived barefoot until his death. He was once asked, "Why do you not buy some sandals?" and he replied, "I do not wish to change the condition in which I entered God's presence." He who is united to God must show courtesy in His presence, mighty and majestic, and not concern himself with deeds, whether few or many, as it is said: "If you are given to understand an aspect of things, let it not occupy your mind, though your good works be few or many." The gnostic must not work to serve something which distracts him from God, as has been said: "Let your gaze take in the beauties of His Face. Therein you will find all beauty manifested."[39] And it was also said: "There is a Countenance which, when beheld, contains all obligatory and voluntary acts of worship." Thus it is ruled for one who is weak. He does not return after arriving and in the same way, he who has revealed his parts, that is, he who finds nothing remaining to him so that his covering falls from him, and who has realities revealed to him in his state of divine attraction need not return either, for this state was given to him and God is pleased with it. He blesses him and causes him to draw near. His tongue spoke of the secrets he perceived and his friends denied him and accused him of speaking falsehoods. All that befell him was due to his loss of his covering, but necessity brings about what takes place and when he does cover up his condition he thereby affirms it, just as a cause is mirrored in its effect, whether it be through its presence or absence. When the author spoke of covering the private parts, saying that it is conditional upon mindfulness and ability, and excludes weakness and forgetfulness, he was referring to the gnostics and lovers of God who were granted a vision of His reality and who spoke of it in inimitable and indescribable terms. Clear explanations are for those who possess a firm station, while mutterings are given by those in a temporary state (of grace). The author then spoke of what was permissible to reveal of this reality, saying:

Save the face and hands of a free woman
all else must be covered, and regarded as private parts.

When he mentions that concealment is obligatory, be it known that the gnostic adopts the greatest concealment, for he is not permitted to glory in the secrets of freedom. He says that this freedom, being contrary to slavehood, is something which is forbidden to reveal, "except the face and hands." Those who are veiled may not have revealed to them anything save the face and the hands; the uncovering of these two parts means the unveiling of certain qualities in order to help man ascend to the Essence, for when the lover beholds an aspect of his Beloved his heart becomes aflame and he gains the strength to attain his goal. And know that the revealing of the hands and face takes place among the truthful, not among those who disturb by their speech, for to see the Beloved without veils is only given to those who show respect. Otherwise her beauty must be veiled, and her sun must be covered by cloud. What protects the majesty of freedom is her veil, and what protects the majesty of the sun is her cloud. Each time the free woman veils herself, she is assailed with pleas; and each time she reveals her face, the whole of existence is illuminated by her beauty, as one of them has said:

> Was it lightning that flashed
> from the side of the mountain
> Or did Layla lift the veils from her face?
> Yes, it was Layla who shone, and by her face
> Day broke, radiating with the light of her beauty.

When her purity is unveiled and her covering raised for those who contemplate her, she then orders them to conceal her light from those who deny its existence, and they undertake to do whatever is needed to veil her (may God be pleased with them!) until they nearly cover her completely out of their wish to preserve her and their jealousy for her, as one of them has said: "I hid her out of jealousy that she be seen." What love belongs to guardianship, and how powerful it is! For when she revealed herself to them, leaving nothing covered, they concealed her and it was as though they saw nothing. One of them has said:

> "Tell us of Layla, for you are her guardian."
> I said to them, "I tell you I am no guardian."

These are the keepers of the message and of the gates to union; therefore, delight, brother, at their side, and submit to their authority, for knowledge may be sought only from their kind, and worship is accepted only from those who keep company with them.

The call to prayer for a group is Sunna at the times of the five obligatory prayers, but not otherwise.

"The call to prayer for a group is *Sunna*" meaning for a group of Sufis who have among them a realized soul; that is, you have gone to them and found among them one unique (*fard*) in his time. The words "at the time" means one who is the master of his era. These have the right to declare themselves by the call and gather together those who seek knowledge, before their time runs out. Time is short, and to perform the prayer on time is better than the whole earth and all that is in it. When we say "unique" (*fard*) we do not mean those who have attained to a station of blessing and righteousness. Taking knowledge from these last belongs to the category of an extra prayer, and the call is not permitted for this type of prayer. The words "at the time" excludes those who do not exist at the time of the prayer, such as the gnostics who have died. Even if they are of the "unique" (*fard*), they are of those who have passed away. The call cannot be made by the latter but only by him who is possessed of both the stations of uniqueness and presentness (*fardan waqtiyyan*). His uniqueness will be indicated by the fact that most of those who join him will also become "unique," that is, they will attain to the station of uniqueness (*fardāniyya*), and by the fact that answering his call will be obligatory for every aspirant, since he will bring knowledge springing from his pact with God and renew man's faith. This renewal is possible only through meeting such men face to face, for they are the beloved of whom the Prophet (peace and blessings be upon him!) spoke: "Renew thy faith by meeting the beloved." The beloved are not those who you love by yourself and by your nature, or on account of their good treatment of you, for those will not renew your faith. The soul is created with a disposition to love him who treats it well, even if he be a disbeliever; but the beloved who renew faith are those of whom the Prophet said, "Submit to my beloved." And he also said to his Companions: "You are my Companions, and they are my beloved." Therefore strive, brother, to know one of his beloved. Show him your love for him until he loves you, for when he loves you know that it is God who loves you and has chosen you for His bounty and made you draw near to Him.

The "unique" one of the present time is rarer than red sulfur.[40] Whoever can find him has found all, for he is of the noblest of stations, as the Prophet (peace and blessings be upon him!) said: "Verily God is Unique and He loves the unique." And he also said, "Persevere on your path, for the unique ones have preceded you." He was asked, "Who are the unique ones, O Messenger of God?" And he replied: "They are those who saw the inner reality of this world while other men saw only its outer shell." Indeed, they saw its inner reality comprising its essences, its substance, and its lights, and saw all this with true vision. The world thus became for them but a great mirage in which the thirsty man thinks to have water but upon approaching it, finds naught save God to be there. When these beloved found God, they remained with Him, abandoning both this world and the next—in truth, they left everything upon reaching Him. Not one of them returned to the world of forms, but all resided in the Spirit.

Know further that this call is also meant for the traveler who comes to arid ground, and by the latter we mean a place which is empty of guidance to this inner reality—it appears then as if it is devoid of any spring or stream. The Prophet (peace and blessings be upon him!) said in praise of such guides: "By them are men given water, and through them do they receive sustenance…."

And it is said:

> Everywhere you go you are welcomed
> As if you were rain for the dry earth
> A gentle glance is sought from you
> You are as a flower in the eyes of men
> Your light guides the traveler to his goal
> You are as the moon in the dark of night.

Man is contained in the universe, but the universe is contained in the gnostic. The rising of the sun of wisdom brings illumination to the heart of the gnostic; each time the sunrise approaches, his morning light is manifest, and when this light gains in strength, it becomes his noon-day sun.

The morning smiles upon the approaching light of day; in the same way, the heart of the gnostic is illumined by the proximity of the Beloved. One who glimpses such light knows the Beloved is close to entering his abode. A place is illumined upon the coming of its inhabitants, and which illumination is dearer to the heart than that which tells of the coming of the Beloved? This is the best of times; there is nothing more beloved or sought after by the gnostics than this time. In it the sun of reality rises over the clouds of created things, and the earth is illumined by the light of her

Lord—the souls on earth are lit up by the rise of the sun of the divine Presence. It is the time of the union of the branches with their root, the time of the joining of that which was separated.

This is indeed the time. All else is but vanity. When the wind of the divine Presence descends and the heart's Beloved draws near, what soul would not be transported? What heart would not yearn to prolong that moment? In union, every prolongation of time seems but a moment in duration, while endless appears every moment in separation.

NOTES

1. Sufis.

2. An opinion arrived at by logical deduction from Quran and *ḥadīth*.

3. See Quran, *Sura al-Wāqiᶜa.*

4. XIII, 4.

5. XXXVIX, 18.

6. XXI, 107.

7. XVII, 20.

8. *The Universal Man* by Abd al-Karim al-Jili.

9. Abu al-Hasan al-Shushtari, d. 1268.

10. The seven verses refers to the *Fatiḥa*, the opening chapter of the Quran which is an essential part of the Muslim canonical prayer.

11. XXII, 73.

12. XVI, 4.

13. II, 115.

14. XXIV, 35.

15. VI, 76.

16. II, 115.

17. VI, 84.

18. VI, 80.

19. XVIII, 110.

20. XLI, 54.

21. LV, 19-20.

22. XXI, 107.

23. One of the Prophet's wives.

24. XII, 84.

25. LVII, 4.

26. XII, 87.

27. XXXVII, 96.

28. Excellence, spiritual virtue. The third and highest of the degrees of faith.

29. *Ḥadīth qudsi.*

30. *Ḥadīth qudsi.*

31. VI, 104.

32. LXX, 19–22.

33. XCVI, 19.

34. LXXIV, 4.

35. II, 222.

36. XLI, 46.
37. Ibn Ata Allah.
38. VII, 201.
39. Umar ibn al-Farid, d. 1235.
40. Red Sulfur is an alchemical symbol and refers to the material that can transform silver into gold; it is used by Sufis as a metaphor indicating an exalted spiritual level.

Treatise on the Invocation of the Divine Name
By The Shaykh al-Alawi

In the Name of God, the Merciful, the Compassionate

Praise be to God, and He is our sufficiency. May He grant peace to His chosen servants. From the servant of his Lord, Ahmad Ibn Mustafa al-Alawi al-Mustaghanimi, to the honorable So-and-so. Peace, mercy, and blessings be upon you. I was honored by your visit accompanied by the beloved Shaykh So-and-so, but I observed during our brief conversation that you felt rancor (or so it seemed to me) against your brethren the Alawites not for any sin they committed, but because they ceaselessly pronounce the unique Name *Allāh*. You feel that this deserves reproof, or let us say chastisement, for according to you, they devote themselves to this Name whether it is appropriate to do so or not; according to you, it does not matter to them if they happen to be in the street in a place that is deemed unsuitable for such an utterance. This is true, you say, to such an extent that when one of them knocks on the door, he says *Allāh*, when someone calls to him, he says *Allāh*, when he stands he says *Allāh*, when he sits he says *Allāh*, and so on.

In addition, you are of the opinion that this Name does not merit being called a form of invocation as it does not, according to you, constitute a complete sentence (*kalām mufīd*), based on what the grammarians have determined as being necessary components of grammatical constructions.

I am answering you concerning all these things solely for the purpose of arriving at an understanding, and in order to determine the correctness of the Alawites' actions.

The question is, is this permissible or not? I write this missive in the hope that it might provide a cure for the heart and rest for the soul.

To begin with, what you say about the grammarian stipulations of necessary components of complete sentences is correct, except that you do not realize that when the grammarians laid down this rule it pertained to the classification of a form of speech that conveys a meaning to the listener. They had no thought of applying this criterion to forms of invocation, of judging its legality or illegality, of discussing the rewards due for accomplishing it, and so on. Were you to have asked them about this in their day or were you to do so today, they would undoubtedly answer by saying, "What we have stipulated in that regard is merely a technical formulation that we use in our field, for such formulations prevent ambiguity of meaning in our discussions." You are well aware of the fact that the formulations used by grammarians differ from those used by theologians, which differ in their turn from those used by doctors of the law, and these differ once again from those used by specialists in the origins of law, and so on. In this way, every group uses its own terminology, which leads us to conclude that the grammarians were for their part concerned with the identification of complete sentences—that speech which benefits the person addressed in some way. They were not concerned with distinguishing lawful invocations from unlawful ones. In other words, conditions about the requirements of grammatical speech are meant in particular for him who wishes, by his words, to inform someone of something. The one who invokes, however, does it only to benefit his soul and in order to establish the meaning of the noble Name firmly in his heart, and other intentions of this kind. Moreover, the grammarians did not formulate these conditions so as to include the expressions of a grieving or saddened man, for the latter's intention is not that of the grammarians. The grammarian would hardly say to him, "I do not understand what you mean by your sighs and groans, for they are not a grammatical statement—they need some explanation," or the like. The intention of the saddened or grieving man is not to inform others of anything, but only to console his heart. In the same way, the intention of one who invokes the Name is to have it become imprinted permanently in his soul.

You know, brother, that every name has an influence that attaches itself to the soul of he who utters it, even if it is not one of the divine Names. For example, if a man repeats the word "death" he will feel an effect which attaches itself to him on account of mentioning this word, especially if he persists in it. This effect will undoubtedly be different from the one had by the mention of "money," "power," or "authority," even without considering this in the light of the noble *ḥadīth*: "Increase in remembrance of the Destroyer of Pleasures" (*Ḥazim al-Ladhdhāt*), the reference here being to death. The word "death" is but one word, yet it is said that among some of the first believers it formed an entire litany. Every man with a sense of the subtle is aware of the effect of what is mentioned on the soul, whether it be something serious or light-hearted. If we admit this, then we are bound to admit also that the Name of God has an influence on the soul, as do other names, each to its own degree. And brother, do not lose sight of the fact that a name is as noble as that which is named, inasmuch as it bears its imprint in the folds of its secret essence and meaning.

Now let us cease to consider everything set forth above, and concern ourselves solely with the judgment of the Lawgiver (God) concerning the pronunciation of this Name: we see that it must fall under one of the five categories of the law, namely the obligatory (*wujūb*), the recommended (*nadb*), the permitted (*ibāha*), the strongly discouraged (*karāha*), and the forbidden (*ḥurma*) for there exists no question pertaining to words or actions that does not fall within one of these categories. Thus, before opposing the utterance of this Name, one should decide under which category such an act falls. If we find that it is something forbidden or strongly discouraged then we are obliged to oppose whoever does it, for he has committed something worthy of reproach. If, on the other hand, it does not fall into either of these categories, then to reproach it is unjust, for the person concerned has uttered something permissible, even if it is not obligatory or recommended and even if it falls just within the bounds of the lawful. What is to prevent us from repeating something lawful, and how can you make the one who does so deserve reproach or punishment through stripping this Name of all religious significance? However we think of this, we cannot classify it among the strongly discouraged or forbidden things, and it retains its value in accordance with its divine station.

You are the type who limits himself to the levels that suit you; and whoso honors that which is sacred to God has done well in the eyes of his Lord; "and whoso honors the commandments of God has acted out of devotion of heart."[1] All that we have thus far set forth has been done for the sake of determining that the Name is unique, and without association with anything, be it even by way of implication. If we search for the truth, stripping it of its veils, we can see that its mention is permitted even for a grammarian, for it is in reality a noun in the vocative[2] which is classified as a complete sentence because it has a vocative particle meaning "I call." It is permissible and even common to omit this particle in Arabic. In fact, very often the position of the words makes it necessary to do this—as for example in the case we are speaking of—because of the demands of Quranic knowledge and Islamic learning which are, perhaps, greater among the Sufi masters than among others.

I sincerely hope, brother, that you do not think it unlikely that people devoted to a Sufi path can realize a manner of acting in conformity with the Quran and persevere in piety to attain to discernment between the true and the false. God has said: "If thou fearest God He will grant thee discernment."[3] These people have yearned in their innermost beings for this and God has given to them what He has withheld from others.

In addition to all that we have said previously about the invocation of the unique Name with the vocative particle omitted, there is the fact that those who invoke thus obey the words of God: "Say: Invoke *Allāh*, or invoke The All Merciful. However ye call upon Him, His are the most beautiful Names."[4] They have thus concentrated upon the first form of invocation ordered by Him. This is our saying *Allāh*. Through their single-minded effort and their total absorption in the solitary invocation of God "standing, sitting, and lying on their sides,"[5] and through their perseverance in the commanded invocation, the triumph of the divine in them compels them to drop the vocative particle, for the latter is used for one who is far, not for Him who is "nearer to us than our jugular vein."[6] There are verses from the Book of God which prove the truth of the inspiration of those who invoke thus. Invocations are of two types: those from the servant to his Lord, and those from God to His servant. There are examples of the first type where the vocative particle has been dropped, and of the second where it has been kept. How is this, I wonder? And how were people guided to do thus? Glory be to God! I would like to quote the great Abu Ishaq al-Shatibi.[7] Let us content ourselves to draw from his words (may he rest in peace!). Citing from his book *al-Muwāfaqāt*, part 2, pp. 68-69: "The Quran contains a call from God to men and from men to God, the glorious, conveyed through stories and teachings. When God calls to man, it is always with a vocative particle because of the distance of the latter, as in His words: 'O my slaves who believe! Verily my earth is vast.'[8] 'Say: O my slaves who have squandered themselves,'[9] 'Say: O mankind! Verily I am the Messenger of God to you all.'[10] 'O ye who believe.'[11] If there is a vocative mentioned from man to God, it appears without the vocative particle, for originally it was used when cautioning someone, and God cannot be cautioned. Moreover, the vocative particles signify distance, for example the particle *yā*—which is the principal one—and God has revealed that He is near to the one who calls upon Him, particulary by His words: 'When my servants question thee concerning Me, then verily I am nigh.'[12] It is also clear in His words to mankind as a whole: 'There is no conversation between three men but He is the fourth, nor between five but He is the sixth.'[13] And, "And we are nearer to him than his jugular vein."[14] From these words men have gained two teachings: one is to drop the vocative particle and the other, to be conscious of the divine immanence. Similarly, in keeping the particle for the previous category, namely that from God to man, there are two significations: firstly it serves to strengthen those who, while having the position of servant, tend to be forgetful, and turn away from God in their blindness. It is also an indication of the elevation of Him who calls upon man and shows that He is far above being "near" as men are, for in His nearness He is exalted, and in His exaltation He is near, glory be to Him! The call of the servant to God is one of yearning and asking for whatever will better his soul. The supplications in the Quran use the expression "Lord" (*rabb*) in most instances, to admonish and teach; for in his supplication the servant should address God using the expression that corresponds to His station, and the word "Lord" means the one who helps those who are under His dominion (*al-marbūb*).

God has clearly set forth the supplications of the servant as follows: "Our Lord, do not take us to task if we forget or err. Our Lord, do not make us bear a burden as you did those who came before us," etc.[15] So you see—may God have mercy on you—that the invocations by the servant omit the vocative *yā* for the reasons set forth above. If you have understood this, then tell me, by your Lord: If we hear the people omitting the vocative *yā* in their invocations and prayers to their Lord, are they still to be reproached? And do they do this because of their understanding of their religion, or because of their complete ignorance thereof?

Given all of our attempts to prove our point, I am yet aware that the opponent, or let us say the one who is searching for the correct answer, will continue to scrutinize the texts and proofs of the other side indicating the legality of invoking the Name alone and showing this practice to come from that of the earliest believers. At the same time, those who are searching thus should not forget that the other side is also curious to see the proofs and arguments which judge the invocation thus to be illegal and say that the earliest believers never used it. The strongest basis you have for this disagreement is the grammatical argument that the

Name is not structured speech. We have shown the falseness of this statement by the proofs in this section; even if there were more texts in your possession concerning this, you should at least not be so quick to reject what people may have as arguments. Finally, whether each side is given an equal voice or not, the matter remains within the realm of *ijtihād*.[16] Thus, the statement of the opponent to the effect that the invocation of this Name in isolation is not permissible proves nothing to those who say the opposite. The crux of the matter is that your assertion of illegality is restricted to what concerns you in particular; but legislating and compelling others to do things is the prerogative of the Infallible, and no one else can say of his own accord, "this is permitted" or "this is not." Whoever does so should lower his voice where his ignorance of the subject exceeds his knowledge. This is a principle that holds for all other disputes, for the Sufi, like others, is obliged to bow his head and to refrain from holding other opinions in the face of the noble law and the holy Book.

It is certainly possible that the opponent will attack us from another quarter, saying that we have no right to worship and seek reward for a practice that we do not know for certain the earliest Muslims performed. To this we would reply, yes, this is as you say. I hope for the sake of God that we are at least in unison on this point. However, I believe you will not forget, brother, and take note that it is in fact permissible to recite the divine Names and this is proven by the words of the Mighty and Powerful: "To God belong the most beautiful Names, so invoke Him by them."[17] They are single words, and although they are thus, neither this verse nor any other have stipulated as to how the invocation should be pronounced—that is, what form it should take, and so on. This, I believe, is simply out of consideration for the levels of those who are pious and on the path of God, for they will vary in strength and weakness, desire and awe, passion and yearning. People are at different levels and there are degrees of desire for God; and the innermost depths of men are known from the standpoint of their relationship with Him, mighty and glorious. From this we see that there were no restrictions concerning the forms of prayers and invocations among the earliest believers that could cause us to conclude that the Name was definitely not used as a form of invocation among them, or that they did not consider this Name as a form of invocation. For we do not know with certainty all that they uttered in their seclusion or in the world, or in times of illness or health. It is impossible for us to believe that the companions of the Prophet (may God be pleased with them!) did not repeat the name of God, *Allāh, Allāh*, for He has protected them from such a possibility. Here I would like to put before you evidence which will decide the argument, and you may see then that this question has a wider import than you imagined. Muslim in his *Saḥīḥ* related on the authority of Abu Hurayrah (may God be pleased with him!) that the latter once saw a sick man groaning in the presence of the Prophet (peace and blessings of God be upon him!). One of the companions told him to cease his groaning and exhorted him to be patient. The Prophet then said, (peace and blessings of God be upon him!) "Let him groan, for he is invoking one of the Names of God most high." Al-Bukhari and Tirmidhi also had on the authority of Abu Hurayrah that the Prophet said, "Let him groan, for the groan is one of the Names of God which brings relief to the ill."[18] Then—God have mercy on you—what would you do in such a situation if the sick man were pronouncing the name of Majesty—*Allāh, Allāh*—instead of saying "*ah!, ah!*"?

Would it be correct for this companion to forbid him this? Certainly not, for the exaltedness of the Name clearly precludes this possibility. The companion was reproached only because of his failure to understand the meaning of the word "*ah*," for it is one of the Names of God most high—and the Prophet (peace and blessings be upon him) acknowledged that it is a form of invocation as such, apart from its being classified as a Name of God. This is undoubtedly a valuable lesson which should make men think well of those who invoke, however they do so. But even supposing you are not convinced that what we have presented to you as a logical argument is sound, yet justice permits one only to say that the question is one about which we must remain in disagreement. However sure its conclusion may seem to us by this argument, it remains a question of *ijtihād* and thus, how can you try to compel us, brother, to agree with your argument or submit to your *ijtihād* when we compel you to nothing of the sort? All this is one thing, and what is more, however much you assail your brethren the Alawites with reproaches, you cannot prevent them from following the way of those who invoke the Name alone, or from advocating this invocation for the leaders and guides of religion.

Here I would like to quote a passage which, God willing, will put your hearts at rest. I am assuming that you have not heard of it before, for, if you had, how could you regard the Alawites with such contempt, since they are among those the saying refers to? In the *Mufīd al-Rāwī* of Shaykh Mustafa Ma'al-Aynayn[19] it is written that Ibn Jarir in his commentary on the Quran spoke of the importance for the aspirant on the path of confining himself solely to the invocation of the unique Name. Shaykh Mustafa said further that when the servant pronounces the word *Allāh* shafts of light rise from within him and spread over the horizon, traveling up until they reach the divine Throne, filling all of creation with their light. At this God says to it, "Cease." And the light replies, "By your might and majesty, I will not cease until you grant forgiveness to the one who utters your Name." He would then say, "By My might and majesty, I have sworn an oath before the creation of the world that I will cause no one to utter this Name except those whose sins I have forgiven."

In his *Sharḥ al-Mubāḥith al-Aṣliyya*, Ibn Ajiba[20] (may God have mercy on him!) relates that Abu Hamid al-Ghazali (may God be pleased with him!) said: "At first I desired to travel upon the path with many prayers, litanies, and fasts. Then, when God saw the sincerity of my intention, He brought me to one of His saints who said to me: 'My son, rid yourself of all preoccupations save God alone. Withdraw into isolation, gather together all your strength and fervor, and say *Allāh, Allāh, Allāh*.'" And al-Ghazali in his *Mishkāt al-Anwār* said: "As long as you occupy youself with that which is other than God, you must remain with the negation, *lā ilāha.*[21] When you have become oblivious to all of creation by your contemplation of Creator, then you have left the negation behind and attained the affirmation: 'Say *Allāh*! Then leave them to their vain talk.'"[22] He also said: "When you have left behind the remembrance of what never was, and devoted yourself to the remembrance of He who has never ceased to be, then when you say *Allāh* you will be delivered from all that is other than God." He also said, "Open the door of your heart with the key of the saying *lā ilāha illa Allāh*, the door of your spirit with the word *Allāh*, and invoke the presence of your innermost essence (*sirr*) with the word *Huwa, Huwa*."[23] Al-Ghazali also said in his work *al-Maqsad al-Ana fī Sharḥ Asmāʾ Allāh al-Ḥuṣnā*, speaking of the divine name *Allāh*, that the servant should derive his sustenance from it, meaning from the invocation (*dhikr*), which deifies the slave; and we mean by this that his heart and aspirations become drowned in God most high, neither seeing nor turning to anything outside of Him. Thus al-Ghazali desired all believers to receive their sustenance from this Name. If you decide to choose what al-Ghazali chose for you, brother, then it is this. And if you do not so choose, do not hope that what you do will act as a proof against those whose choice agrees with that of al-Ghazali.

Even if we were to grant that your arguments could bear some weight against such as the Alawites, could you also argue against our forebearers, some of whom were scholars and Quranic interpreters, such as Fakhr al-Din al-Razi and others?[24] For he himself undertook the practice of the invocation of the Name and clearly expressed his choice in his *al-Tafṣīr al-Kabīr*, in the section on the *Basmala*, where he says: "Know, O people, throughout my life I repeat the word *Allāh*. When I die I will say *Allāh*, when I am questioned in the grave I will say *Allāh*, on the Day of Resurrection I will say *Allāh*, when I take the book I will say *Allāh*, when my good and bad deeds are weighed I will say *Allāh*, when I reach the path I will say *Allāh*, when I enter Paradise I will say *Allāh*, when I see God I will say *Allāh*, etc." Al-Razi said all this in spite of the contempt of those who do not say *Allāh*. We took pains to transmit these lines so that you may realize, brother, that the Alawites are not inventing something by their invocation of the word *Allāh*, as you suspected. We hope you will also realize that the generality of Sufis share this practice with them, and believe that this Name is the supreme one. If the Most High is called by it, He will surely answer, and if something is requested of Him through this Name, it will be given. And this belief is not confined to the Sufis alone, but extends to more than one religious leader, as well as to the majority of transmitters of *ḥadīth* and theologians. Concerning this, Shaykh Muhammad Bayram the fifth[25] (may God have mercy on him!), who enjoins the invocation of the Divine Name, said: "It was related in the *Radd al-Muḥtār*[26] that Hisham said on the authority of Muhammad Ibn abu Hanifah (may God be pleased with him!) '*Allāh* is the supreme Name of God most high.'" Al-Tahawi[27] said the same, as well as many other religious scholars. Shaykh Abu Muhammad Abd al-Qadir ibn Yusuf al-Fasi[28] also cited it among his arguments in defense of the legality of invoking the divine Name by itself. He then said: "In the *Saḥīḥ* it says, 'The Last Hour will not come until there no longer remains anyone on earth who says *Allāh, Allāh*.'" This is excellent evidence in a single sentence in favor of the mention of this word by itself, and is transmitted either as *Allāhu, Allāhu*, in the nominative; or in the accusative case as *Allāha, Allāha*. One can undeniably pronounce the noble Name alone, and this being so, how can one object to someone repeating it often, and what would be the nature of his objection? The preceding *ḥadīth* was related by the Imam[29] in his *Musnad* and by Ibn Maja in his *Saḥīḥ* from Anas ibn Malik (may God be pleased with him!) thus: "The Last Hour will not come until the time when *Allāh, Allāh* is no longer invoked on earth." The greatest proof, as I have indicated, is from this *ḥadīth*, for in it the divine Name is repeated, and this shows clearly that He wishes us to invoke the Name. If the passage had the Name written only once it could have been construed as "until there no longer remains anyone on earth who believes in the existence of *Allāh*." However, because it is repeated, there is no such implication.

Let us assume that the divine law contains no indication whatsoever as to whether the repetition of the Name is permitted or not. If this is the case, then there is nothing at all to cause one to prohibit its repetition by the tongue, or its passage to the heart. In fact, it appears that there is nothing in the law to forbid the repetition of any name related by tradition and if this is so, then how can pronouncing one of the divine Names be prohibited? Far be it from the divine law to contain such excesses and deviation and oblige the believer not to repeat the Name of his Lord—not to say *Allāh, Allāh*, or what is the same, not to repeat any of the rest of God's Names, for He said: "To God belong the most beautiful Names, so call upon Him by them"[30] meaning petition Him by them and invoke Him by them. This is what we have understood and chosen for ourselves. You in turn have the right to choose for yourselves, but you should not oblige us to agree with your choice while we have not obliged you to agree with ours. I will end this section by quoting a passage that contains conclusive proof about the matter. I say this assuming the humility and generosity of those who claim that this Name is in the category of strongly discouraged things. I ask forgiveness of God! The question of the strongly discouraged (*karāha*) or permitted (*nadab*) category of the word has been resolved, and it was stipulated that it ranks above the merely "permissible." Concerning this, al-Ajhuri, in his *Sharḥ* of Khalil mentions the following on the authority of al-Mawwaq: "If there is a disagreement as to whether something is 'permitted' or 'strongly discouraged,' it is better to do it than not to. In the same way, if there is disagreement as to whether an action is part of the *Sunna*, or strongly discouraged, then it cannot be less than 'permitted' in any case."

All the passages that we have set forth here are intended to act as intercessors on our behalf, so that you accept the excuses of the Alawites for whatever wrong they have committed by the invocation of the divine Name—and may God accept the excuses of all, Amen! All that has been said thus far refers to the first question, namely the legality or illegality of invoking the Name.

You also mentioned, or let us say objected, to the fact that they repeatedly utter the name of Majesty whether or not it is appropriate to do so. They behave thus in the street and other such places. It appears to you that this attitude is lacking in reverence for the divine Names, and that this practice was never specifically ordered by the law. When one of them knocks on the door, he says *Allāh*, when someone calls to him he says *Allāh*, and other things of this kind, all of which you find inappropriate. Here I must add that however indulgent I am in my answer I am yet compelled, after asking your leave, to say that you have neglected to reveal the *ḥadīths* relevant to our case which have given you cause to reproach the Alawites for having done something wrong. For, if you had indeed read about such traditions you would not have tried to oppose us on the basis of suspicions that the earliest believers practiced differently. If you were able to find texts which corroborate what we have said, I am certain that you would have scrutinized them and pondered them in your heart, submitting to what they say, and placing them above your own opinion. This is only proper and fitting for someone in your position. Thus, here I will quote what should be sufficient, God willing, to show that in the practice of the Alawites free, spontaneous invocation is not outside the realm of the *Sunna*; nor is it in conflict with it. We have concluded that it is the essence of the *Sunna*, and we base this belief on the command to "practice the invocation"; this must indicate that it is not to be restricted to a certain time or place, but can be practiced at all times and in all places. At each instant, man must build upon his moments of remembrance and rid himself of his inherent forgetfulness so that the former gains strength in his mind and remains fixed in his consciousness. In other words, the remembrance of God is praiseworthy whatever the circumstances, just as forgetfulness is blameworthy whatever the circumstances. Certainly the best course for both of us is to seek direction from the holy Book and the *Sunna.* The passages which the Quran contains about the importance of the invocation and its warnings about being forgetful probably do not need to be quoted for clarification, especially to such as you. The *Sunna*, in turn, contains passages which are no less clear, but it will not hurt for us to quote a few of these *ḥadīths*, along with some practices established by the four schools of law, so that we know the Will of the Lawgiver concerning us, and can act according to it, God willing. Ibn Durays and Abu Yala[31] related on the authority of Abu Said al-Khudri: "It is incumbent upon you to fear God as much as possible, and to mention His Name at every tree and stone." The most important idea here is the generalization of time and place with reference to the practice of the invocation. Similarly, Imam Ahmad in his *Muṣnad* related on the authority of Anas, through a faultless chain of transmission that the Messenger of God (peace and blessings be upon him!) used to invoke at every free moment. Aisha related the same tradition. Al-Alqama[32] transmitted from al-Dimiri that the Prophet (peace and blessings be upon him!) invoked God while performing the ablution, when in conversation, and when standing, lying down, walking, or on horseback, etc. Nawawi relates something similar in his commentary on *Muslim*, the gist of which is that the Prophet (upon him be blessings and peace!) constantly practiced the invocation, regardless of circumstance or place. Anyone who researches legal opinions of scholars on this subject will find ample evidence indicating unanimous consensus in favor of this invocation. The Hanafi masters have related according to the *Nujūm al-muhtadīn*, that the Qadi Khan said: "The invocation of God, as well as irreligious and dispersive gathering are permitted in the market place, provided that the one in the first activity is preoccupied with glorifying and declaring the oneness of God, and the others are preoccupied with their worldly affairs." If you ponder—God have mercy on you!—the words "dispersive and irreligious gatherings" you will find that the Alawites are not so negligent as to belong to that category. In fact, the invocation has even been permitted in the hot baths, the place where one's private parts are uncovered and one cleanses oneself of filth. This is shown in a large number of texts such as: "Reciting the Quran out loud while in the bath is disliked, but it is not disliked to do so in a whisper, just as one can glorify God and pronounce the testimony of unity there, even in a loud voice." Other statements like this are to be found among the Hanafi masters in such works as the *Fatāwa al-Khāniyya*, the *Husāmiyya*, the *Sīrājiyya*, the *Mutalaffaẓ*, and the *Jinas*. The author of the *Nuṣra* also quoted something similar. If the invocation is permissible in the bath, what is the sin if the Alawites invoke in the street, for example? Given that a person unaccustomed to hearing someone invoke in such places may be repulsed by it, it is nonetheless incumbent upon the impartial man, if he wishes to judge others, to do so according to the justice of God and His prophets and not according to what he would choose or approve by himself. He should act without fear of the man who approves of one thing and disapproves of all other possibilities. For this reason, we must not be concerned with what a few have approved of, but should limit ourselves to choosing one of the possibilities contained in the religious law. The duty, then, for all who believe in God and the Last Day, is to look no further than these texts, and to act in accordance with their commands by choosing for their soul what God chooses for it. "When God and His Messenger ordain something for the believer, whether man or woman, it is not proper for him to choose for himself in the matter."[33]

Brother, in spite of the nobility of your intention to examine this question by means of texts and statements of scholars, perhaps what we have quoted here will suffice you, though but a summary. If you need more evidence—and the believer often needs an increase in what is good—I will say further that more than one religious leader has clearly stated that the invocation is permitted even in the toilet. We mention this to make you recall that you even considered permitting invocation in the street to be something unthinkable. The Qadi Iyad[34] in the conclusion of his *Kitāb al-Ṣalāt* said: "The legal schools of Abd Allah ibn Amr ibn al-As, Shafii, Malik, and Ibn Bashir all permit the invocation of God most high in the toilet, etc." It is also indicated in Ibn Rushd's[35] *Samāʾ Sahnūn* and by Shaykh Muhammad al-Kattani[36] in his quotation of Burzuli's treatise on the explanation of the words of God: "O ye who believe! Enter not houses other than your own without first asking permission to enter, and saluting those within."[37] The permitted nature of the invocation is also indicated in the *Sunan al-Muhtadīn*[38] as follows: "Al-Lakhami said, 'He who is about to relieve himself invokes God before entering the place where he does it.'" Iyad,[39] speaking of the permissibility of invoking in the toilet says: "Some have said it is permissible to invoke while relieving oneself and these include Malik, Nakha, and Abd Allah ibn Amr ibn al-As." He also said, "Ibn al-Qasim used to say 'Praise be to God!' if he happened to sneeze while urinating and all of the preceding treatises mentioned this as well." You may ask, "Did not Shaykh Khalil[40] say, 'The invocation of God should be avoided when in the toilet'?" and it was in fact said that one should refrain from it. Perhaps at first glance it appears that the words of Ibn Abd al-Salam[41] and Khalil indicate that something one should refrain from doing must fall into the category of the forbidden. We would say that where it can be understood from the words of these men that to refrain from something means that it is forbidden (*harām*), it can equally be understood from Ibn Rushd, Iyad, and the author of the *Tirāz*[42] that the meaning of refraining is that the action is to be strongly discouraged (*makrūḥ*). This is the obviously what is meant in the writings of Jazuli[43] and the author of the *Madkhal.*[44] Some religious leaders, among them Abu Abd Allah al-Hattab,[45] have found fault with those who have understood the word to mean forbidden. He said: "It is not obvious, since none of the statements of earlier sources agree with this meaning, and it has not been declared to mean this. The import of their words should be taken to be 'strongly discouraged' and not 'forbidden,' so as to agree with the earlier sources."

In drawing upon all these texts my purpose is not to favor the legal schools which either permit the invocation in the toilet or otherwise, but in order to demonstrate, brother, that some religious leaders have approved of the invocation even in the place considered to be the worst and most unclean by far. Thus, if you happen to find someone invoking God while in such a place, do not consider it strange, or look upon him as an innovator, for al-Shafii and Malik have stated it to be permitted, and they are sufficiently good examples of those who hold fast to the bond with God and to the *Sunna* of His Messenger (peace and blessings be upon him!). This and other texts clearly declare without a doubt that the Alawites were wronged by your accusations, for they have not gone, through imprudence, to the extreme limits of what is permitted. You have not heard any one of them say that he did not refrain from invocation even in the toilet or in other such unclean circumstances. The most that one can relate of the Alawites is that if someone calls to one of them he says *Allāh* and if he calls out to someone he says *Allāh*, and so on. Someone may say that the Names of God are too exalted to be used as a means of gaining access to anything outside of the realm of the after-life, nor should it be permitted to use them as a means of calling upon someone or attracting his attention. This would be correct, were it not for the fact that this same thing is permitted and even commanded in the religious law. If you were to look in the most obvious area for material which corroborates these arguments, you would find that what God wills of us in this matter is so clear that it comes close to being an order from Him. For example, just consider the call to prayer. As I am sure you know, it has been established as a means of declaring that the times of prayer have come, and as an exhortation to all to fulfill their duty of prayer. It would be more precise and fitting, perhaps, to call out "The time of prayer has come" or "The time for prayer has commenced," or something that indicates the same thing. Why, in that case, is the whole testimony of faith recited and not simply a few words summarizing it? Furthermore, would you have asked why these Names of God have come to be used as instruments to call men to prayer? A similar example is saying "Glory be to God!" to inform the leader in prayer of a mistake, or to inform him of whatever necessity demands. It is said that the companions of the Prophet (may God be pleased with them!) used to awaken each other by the saying, "God is most great!" This is confirmed in both *Ṣaḥīḥ* collections in the story of the valley, where they slept past the time for the dawn prayer, and the first to awaken was Abu Bakr. Umar was the fourth one to awake, and he began calling out "God is most great!" until the Prophet (peace and blessings be upon him!) awoke. Consider—may God have mercy on you!—how they used forms of invocation to awaken one another from sleep. This was how they acted in time of war or otherwise—indicating things by saying "God is most great!" In Khalil's account, Ibn Rushd related something along the same lines: "Boasting is permitted when shooting arrows, at naming ceremonies, and in the battle-cry, but the remembrance of God is better." In addition Ibn Arafah[46] said, "One may boast when he thinks he has hit the mark, but to invoke God is best," etc. Consider how he chose to use the invocation of God as a means of announcing that he hit the mark. They chose thus so as to be in conformity with the will of God, who intended the invocation to be done in every circumstance.

As it is likely that what we have thus far presented is not sufficient to provide a clear enough proof for you concerning the invocation, I thought to quote a few words from *ḥadīth*, especially in connection with the question of invoking God, mighty and powerful, when asking permission to enter someone's home. By this means our noble brother may find the answer to the question which has sent him delving into the texts of religious law. Among those *ḥadīths* which are very clear on the subject is the following: The Prophet (peace and blessings be upon him!) said, "When you reach the doors of your houses, announce your presence by invoking God." This was related by the distinguished al-Sanusi,[47] author of the *ᶜAqāᵓid*, in his book *Nuṣra al-Faqīr* as a response to Abu al-Hasan al-Saghir. This practice is supported all the more by the majority of Quranic exegetes, who have written about the meaning of asking permission before entering in reference to the passage in the Quran: "O ye who believe! Enter not houses other than you own without first asking permission and greeting those within." Fakhr al-Din al-Razi, in his *Tafsīr*, after speaking of a number of aspects of asking permission, says: "Akrama said it means to declare 'God is most great!' and 'Glory be to God!' and other invocations of this kind." Nisaburi,[48] in his exegesis entitled *Gharīb al-Qurᵓān* has the same as al-Razi. Ibn Abu Shaybah, Tirmidhi, Ibn Abu Hatim, Ibn Mardawayh, and Tabarani all relate the authority of Abu Ayyub that he said: "I said, O Messenger of God, tell me about the words of God, 'until you ask permission and greet those within.' The greeting we have learned, but what is the form of asking permission? He replied: 'A man should say "Glory be to God!" "God is great!" or "Praise be to God!" and clear his throat, so that the people within the house hear.'" Al-Suyuti[49] related this *ḥadīth* in his book *al-Durr al-Manthūr fī Tafsīr al-Qurᵓān bi al-Maᵓthūr*. There is no question, among religious leaders, that the invocation is preferable to calling out, or knocking loudly on the door.

Brother, no matter how much you endeavor to examine what we have presented impartially, you should realize that when you create a rift between the *Sunna* and ourselves, it makes us guilty of a form of innovation. For this reason we have risen to combat it with no consciousness or knowledge save that which God inspired in us—He who guides us along with you, Amen!

Before we end this letter, a letter that, God willing, contains blessings for you and for us—I would like to relate some *ḥadīths* on this subject. I hope that you will give them the attention they deserve, as is your custom. There are two *ḥadīths* which contain the essence of all we have said about the duty of devoting oneself to the remembrance of God, mighty and glorious, at every time and place and of filling up every moment with this remembrance. The first is related by Imam Ahmad, Abu Dawud, Ibn abi al-Dunya, Nasai, and Ibn Habban. In Abu Dawud's words: "The Prophet (peace and blessings be upon him!) said, 'Whoever sits in a place and does not invoke God there, his sitting is vain and frivolous in the eyes God.'" There Hafiz Abd al-Azim said the word *al-tira*, pronounced with a short *i* and a single *r*, means a fault and something which God counts against a person. The second *ḥadīth* comes from Abu Dawud and al-Hakim, on the authority of Abu Hurayra (may God be pleased with him!). He said: "No one will arise from a group in conversation where God has not been mentioned except they will be like the corpses of donkeys, and will lament their deed on the Day of Judgment."

Here we end our letter. All victory is in the hands of Him to whom we shall return, and with whom is the final abode. Peace and blessings be upon our lord Muhammad, and upon his family and companions. Praise be to God, Lord of the worlds.

Notes

1. XXII, 30, 32.

2. An example of this is the opposition by some people to those who draw out the final *h* of the word *Allāh*, saying that here the *h* is interrogative, but an interrogation can only exist in complete sentences. Here it has been introduced into a single word, and thus it constitutes a vocative. Ibn Malik in his *Khulāsa* said: "The vocative has a remote object (signified by) *Yā* and *Ay* and *Aa*, and by *Ayyā* and *Hayyā*." Even if we assume it (the divine Name) to be a sentence, no one could object to saying that the implication here is "O God, have mercy on us and forgive us" and the like.

3. VIII, 29.

4. XVII, 110.

5. IV, 103.

6. See Quran, L, 16.

7. d. 1388.

8. XXIX, 56.

9. XXXIX, 53.

10. VII, 158.

11. II, 104.

12. II, 186.

13. LVIII, 7.

14. L, 16.

15. II, 286.

16. Lit. "striving." The exercise of reason by an individual or group in order to form an opinion about a point not explicitly laid down in Quran or *ḥadīth*.

17. VII, 180.

18. At the time this *ḥadīth* was written down they ascribed the wrong source to it. The truth is that al-Rafii Imam al-Din related it in his *Tārīkh al-Qarawīn* on the authority of Aisha and al-Aziz confirmed its reliability.

19. Born end of eighteenth century.

20. d. 1809.

21. The two parts of the first Shahadah, or testimony of faith, are *lā ilāha*—there is no god, *illa Allāh*—save God.

22. VI, 91.

23. "He," the name of the Essence.

24. d. 1210.

25. d. 1889.
26. Written by Ibn Abidin, d. 1836.
27. d. 933.
28. Possibly the son of seventeenth century Shadhili Shaykh Yusuf al-Fasi.
29. Imam Ahmad Ibn Hanbal.
30. VII, 180.
31. d. 1131.
32. Seventh century.
33. XXXIII, 36.
34. d. 1149.
35. Averroes, d. 1198.
36. d. 1927.
37. XXIV, 27.
38. By al-Mawwaq.
39. Qadi Iyad.
40. d. 1365.
41. d. ca. 1262.
42. By Ahmad b. Muhammad al-Khafaji, d. 1659.
43. d. 1465.
44. By Ibn al-Hajj al-Abdari, d. 1336.
45. d. 1546.
46. d. 1401.
47. d. ca. 1490.
48. d. 1328.
49. d. 1505.

A gathering of disciples at Mostaganem.

Selections from the *Dīwān* of the Shaykh al-Alawi

O You Who Interrogate Me

O you who interrogate me, you will be responsible
For whatever consequence our answer may cause!

Here is a detailed answer for you,
Revealing the secrets of the inebriated:

To every thing an access, a way
To every essence a sign, a quality.

To every truth, a proof
And to each thing sincere, firm constancy.

For every lover a beloved,
For every servant a master.

My condition is indeed unique,
And you behold it, bewildered.

Whatever you see of us is pure illusion
For you know not my essence—
It is far beyond you!

It appears to you that I am the one talking
About the attributes of Allah.

All exaltation of us is feeble,
And to compare us to others is to belittle us.

What you know of me is that I am beautiful.
Upon al-Alawi the Essence has made Its Print.

Great is the distance between us,
As between the living and the dead.

My condition is a mystery to you, still inaccessible.
But to think well of it brings your salvation.

Comprehension of us will always fall short,
How often the mind's power fails!

You Who Dwell in Me

You who dwell in me,
In God's name, hasten not
O generous ones, treat gently your dwelling.

Welcome, welcome to you
In whom my heart and mind are enraptured!

May love leave me with no escape,
That I may see none but you in the world.

Is he not in error who sees other than you?
And to commit such a sin is not our intent.

We wish only to forsake everything,
And leave no space for anyone else but you.

This, my friend, is for the folk of divine union,
For they are the wanderers,
Having annihilated the world,

Their families and their ties they left behind
Once they realized the hidden meaning of creation.

They realized that every manifestation
Is rooted in the Origin,
As the wave disappears
In the immensity of the ocean.

When the sun comes up, all the stars fade.
The moon is seen only in obscurity.

So it is for the sages when Layla appears,
For then the illusion of the two worlds fades.

Her appearance requires them to isolate themselves
From the elite as well as from the common.

Their station is blameless, pure
And their state needs no description.

And when they pray, the All is their *qibla.*[1]
Wherever they go their desire is met,

In clarity and splendor they contemplate the True
And their nearness to Him is everlasting.

When they drink, the bitter becomes sweet,
And their language is ambrosial and imbued with perfection.

Everything bows to their power,
In their presence the True One abides.

May they rejoice, for they have attained Divine Favor,
They live in joy, drawing profit from everything,

For the Peerless One has called them unto Him,
And they have responded with the best of responses.

Vessels of Love

Vessels of love are passed among the masters,
Annihilating them, state by state.

O noble men, I said, do you accept me?
Young man, they replied
On condition you be empty!

I hear you well, O noble ones
Still, I implore you, have mercy on my state!

The truth is, there is but pain in me
And feeble are my deeds!

Before you I am nothing,
Yet it is on you that my hopes rest.

The mention of your names
Is wine to my soul,
And your love is my fortune!

I have a burning passion for you
O, that it may abide in me!

O days lost in vanity, senseless…

Had this been my goal from the start,
I would certainly have left all else behind

And wandered, a prey to my passion
Welcomed by the True One.

In love for you there is no blame,
And any other blame I welcome.

It is enough if I possess, among you,
This sublime station.

O Seeker of the Secret, Surrender

O you seeker of the secret, surrender,
Do not disapprove of us.

Leave behind your knowledge and come forth,
That you may take from us.

Had you known before coming across me,
You would not have needed us.

By God! Our knowledge is priceless—
Do not consider it worthless.

If you say you are a resolute seeker,
That which you are looking for is truly with us.

But if you see in others this power,
Turn to them, it will lighten our burden!

By God, he who has tasted the secret
Will judge in our favor.

In it I am indeed the foremost—
Truly the glory therein is ours!

I reveal nothing nor hide anything,
Thus it is between them and me.

We give wisdom and do not withhold
To him who has a share in us.

Through this path we hope to find peace,
And our Lord suffices for us.

The evil of the *nafs*[2] its way He knows,
That it may have no hold on us.

May Your Blessings O Lord and Your Peace
Be on the spirit of our Prophet,

And every venerable one
Among the people of Medina.

The Vanishing of the Veil

The veils vanished
When my Beloved One appeared.
O lovers of the Precious One,
This is the moment of True Vision.

Let him who desires to partake
Of our hidden secret
Come forth and learn.
He will be shown wisdom—
What an excellent drink!
Its cup bearer calls:
O lovers of the Precious One,
This is the moment of awakening!

It is through this wine[3] that those
Gifted with discernment became conscious.
They have tasted this beverage
From its holder who has filled the vessels
Of this ancient and rich drink
That plunges the lover into rapture.
O lovers of the Precious One,
This is the moment of True Vision.

The master of this wine poured a round
Among the inebriated
And the veils have been torn asunder.
What can he who is veiled understand?
The poor man, so much pain has he given me
He cannot attain to this wisdom.
O lovers of the Precious One,
This is the moment of True Vision.

Enslaved by Love

The beauty of Layla
Has enslaved me

And the heart is lost
With her beauty

Tears flow without cease
Down my face

Her arrows pierced me
And made me ill

With no goal to tend to,
I tend toward none but her

And in the world
She has none like me

O young man, said she,
Slowly! Come…

Approach me with respect
And quench your ardent thirst!

Her discourse increased
My bewilderment

And had it not been for the glass of wine
That allows union…

I understood her words,
I was quick in grasping them

Through an allusion, a smile

With no need of proof

We profited greatly
And we stayed together

Between sobriety and inebriation
For long hours

I kept the veil
That was hiding my intimate one

For fear the unworthy
Should approach with his venom

Upon you be Peace, said I,
O Layla

And on the assembly of noble souls
Who have allowed me this union

O Source of Peace
Bless with beautiful blessing

Him who is a light in the darkness:
Taha,[4] our protector.

O Loved Ones

O loved ones, your favor is all I seek
My love for you ever increases
And has possessed me.
You are my dearly beloved,
Your spirit has made me drunk
And my heart refuses to forget our encounter.
You have conquered my heart; take it as my offering!
The sleepless nights I am left with
Bear witness to my love
You are my ideal, my desire, my elixir, my inebriation,
You who hold my love
Who else could I have equal to you?
You are my sustenance, my refuge
My goal, my support,
You who are most worthy of relation.
Rejoice! Rejoice!
How abundant is the radiance
That fills you during *Dhikr*!
When the singer chants the Name of your Master!
Respond to this *Dhikr*! Let us see you
Drunk and immersed
He Who Calls has called you
You gently aspire to the Truth
And gently It came to you.
You have forsaken all that perishes
And abandoned everything else
In the tumult of life the Lord has preserved you
In the Holy Presence, you have unfurled your flag
Thank the Lord without end,
And may He guard you.
O you who hold the secret, my heart yearns for you!
All along my journey I have adored none but you
Your contentment with me is the great hope of my life.

These Men Who Have Vanished

These men who have vanished in The Divine Presence,
Verily they have melted like snow.

Amazed in their contemplation of God, you see them
Truly inebriated therein.

You see them become drunk at the mention of Allah
The Divine Presence shines upon them

Of the Beauty of God the singer chants,
They rise up on hearing to glorify Him

Their breath is a light wind from God,
Their life subsists with the very Life of God,

Their hearts revolve around God's Mercy
Truly overflowing secrets.

Great intellects, captured by The Divine Dominion,
Souls humbled in their quest for God

They are the fortunate through their bondage to God,
They are the most pious.

He who sees them has witnessed those
Who act through none but Him—
They are divine guides among men

May God's Mercy and His Bliss be upon them,
May the perfume of His Presence be with them.

Dhikr is the Source of All Good Things

Dhikr is the source of all good things.
So reckless was I, so much time did I waste.
Those days are forever gone; what to do now?
Let us, from now on, take advantage of the time,
And sincerely remember God,
And be present through the heart
And through the mind
Dhikr is far better than trade
Ah! If I told you what it is worth:
It is worth more than a kingdom and its ministers.
But people are distracted and neglect it.
This whole world is a waste—
It has invaded both the just and the unjust
May God protect us from its heat!

I fear lest my soul become a mount for this world,
And in its hands I remain captive
After receiving Divine Assistance and noble virtues
Dhikr is the source of all good things.

O Lord! Misfortune has spread everywhere,
And *Dhikr* has become a heavy burden on the tongues.
People have embraced strange ways,
Their conditions, too, are many and varied.
The One Sought is hidden in the seeking,
For sincerity is so rare.
Men's hearts are hard
Good advice profits not those in sin.
I am weary of warning—
What are my words
Compared to those of the Prophets?
Dhikr is the source of all good things.

The sleeping can be awakened,
But he who is dead has no feeling.
Preaching to a dead soul makes no sense—
I would be building a house on the sand.
Men's behavior may lead to insanity—
They are tempting God's Wrath, they rush to doom
A mighty judgment awaits them.

Judgment Day, what a tragedy!
If only you knew what will happen.
If I told you, you would flee from sin!
  Dhikr is the source of all good things.

O brothers, let us repent
And together remember our Lord in prayer!
In the other world, that is all we will find,
And time is so precious,
Let us not waste it!
The damned one will be judged by God,
Refusing to listen,
He does not want to obey.
He disobeys his Lord, committing great sins.
Reminders to the believer are helpful and healing,
They strengthen both his heart and conscience.
He will emerge in great honor,
After being disgraced by sin.
  Dhikr is the source of all good things.

O Lord! Help our community do good and seek virtue,
Abrogate evil acts with good ones,
Grant Your servants Your Pardon,
For us and Your living creatures.
Your Clemency is needed—

Of our evil we repent and turn to you, Almighty!
So many evil acts did I commit,
In public and in secrecy.
And yet, people think I am well—
Had Your Grace not overwhelmed me
And manifest itself in me…
    Dhikr is the source of all good things.

You have made our words facts,
They are recorded in books,
They manifest themselves in people like a sweet breeze.
They capture hearts and souls—
Every noble man desires them.
O My Lord, conceal our blemishes
Al-Alawi has hope,
My Merciful One! Come to our rescue at the time of death
In the name of the Bearer of good news
Come to me, to those present, and to all sincere!
    Dhikr is the source of all good things.

O Muhammad, God Has Chosen You

O Muhammad, God has chosen you
With my heart I praise you
For my tongue is unable to do so—
Indeed, describing my Beloved is beyond my grasp.

I wish to glorify you, O Taha,
But no words can describe you
Expressions of praise cannot encompass at all
Your true worth.
It is vain to describe you,
Just like the stars in the sky—
My feeble sight cannot reach you,
    Yet, from afar, you appear to my eyes.

Elevated like the Pleiades, you are a twinkling star.
O Muhammad, God has chosen you,
With my heart I praise you
For my tongue is unable to do so—
Describing my Beloved is beyond my grasp.

If only this community knew you,
They would devote their lives
To your praise.
In you there is wealth without striving.
Lost is he who chooses other than you
The entire earth and sky
The Throne and the *Qalam*,[5]
All are from your light—
    Here, my reason fails me!

What can I say about him who has
Ascended to the Heavens?
O Muhammad, God has chosen you,
With my heart I praise you
For my tongue is unable to do so—
Describing my Beloved is beyond my grasp.

God's Light is incomparable—
Inability to describe it is true wisdom.
Presumptuous it would be if I dared to do so.
Still, I can say a word:
He has surpassed everything, in depth and height
He was sent as a Mercy to all.
    I have put my trust in him, and God is my witness.
Humble, submissive, and in need,
O Muhammad, God has chosen you,
With my heart I praise you
For my tongue is unable to do so—
Describing my Beloved is beyond my grasp.

Denying the truth does not increase courage—
Without you, I would have never
Known the Almighty,
Nor religion, nor prayer, nor direction.
Your grace has manifested and embraced us,
Through it I have gained might and fame
One earth as in the heavens, I am made proud.
    I am drowned in your love.

My heart throbs, my tears flow.
O Muhammad, God has chosen you,
With my heart I praise you
For my tongue is unable to do so—

Describing my Beloved is beyond my grasp.
The Lord of creation has blessed you,
O master of all masters!
I desire you with fervor
This praise is my plea:
I hope for a path to you
And for my family,
And the poor in God
The day of death and in the grave.
    The believers, too, have hope in your grace.

My heart is so weak, and fears torment it.
O Muhammad, God has chosen you,
With my heart I praise you
For my tongue is unable to do so—
Describing my Beloved is beyond my grasp.

Where would be my dwelling?
How would I be received?
After separation, God knows best.
O Abul Qassem![6] I fear that confusion
Should overwhelm me on the terrible day.
Forgive me, O Imam of messengers!
God forbid that you should forsake the weak.
    I trust you will forgive me,
Old age has afflicted me and
These times are bitter.
O Muhammad, God has chosen you,
With my heart I praise you
For my tongue is unable to do so—
Describing my Beloved is beyond my grasp.

I trust you so much—
Impossible that you would desert me!
Still the burden of my sins frightens me.
How often did I disobey!
O Lord, have mercy on Ben Aliwa,[7]
Deliver him from the sorrows of this world—
At every instant the unexpected appears.

I cannot trust this fickle heart of mine;
O Muhammad, God has chosen you,
With my heart I praise you
For my tongue is unable to do so—
Describing my Beloved is beyond my grasp.

My Tears Flow in Abundance

My tears flow in abundance,
They weary my eyes

O soft evening breeze!
Carry my greetings to Taha…

Transmit to him my salutation, O breeze of union!
Mention to him the torment
His love has caused…

Enchanted by him!
Impossible, I cannot endure this separation
From his dazzling beauty!

O soft evening breeze!
Carry my greetings to Taha…

The light of the beloved, O lover,
Attracts you to its bosom with no escape!
Should he with a fine intelligence perceive it
He would marvel at it, delighted

Indescribable marvel!
He will know It who attains it

He will grasp its sense
Who achieves this union!

O soft evening breeze!
Carry my greetings to Taha…

Follow then this Path, O you
Who desire to approach him!

Follow the guide who will lead you
Towards the Presence of the Prophet

Beware not to deviate
From the path of Love

You will taste a sweet beverage
Ah, what a wine you will be poured!

O soft evening breeze!
Carry my greetings to Taha…

He who serves wine in the Holy Presence
Is none but Taha, the Imam

He will make you forget even the wine he offers you!
Do not blame me if I say

That he is the vessel itself!
The Light of Beauty covering all things…

O soft evening breeze!
Carry my greetings to Taha…

Splendor of the Essence, Muhammad "the Guide"
Radiance of the Divine Attributes

My treasure, my sustenance
My comfort and support at the time of death

On the Day of Judgment
He is the only intercessor!

O soft evening breeze!
Carry my greetings to Taha…

He will indeed intercede
In favor of my followers!

This is my conviction,
Total is my trust

In the chosen one, who is my fortress
On the Day of Judgment

I hope for the Mercy of The Lord

O soft evening breeze!
Carry my greetings to Taha…

I have none but him! At the time of the trial
In him alone rest my hopes

What a glorious station is his!
Muhammad is my hoarded treasure!

My heart is full of love for him
Throughout my life

His grace ceases not
To cover all men

O soft evening breeze!
Carry my greetings to Taha…

O Disciple, Victory is Yours!

O disciple, victory is yours!
Hurry, go toward the One you love

If you desire to annihilate yourself in Him,
Do not listen to anyone but Him.

Let your heart be present in His Name
Visualize it and understand its secret.

Direct your face to none but Him—
It is for Him you quiver with desire.

Cast down your eyes in His Presence
And look within yourself—you will see Him.

You are far from His Beauty,
And yet you are none other than He!

Should they ask: what are you speaking of?
Openly declare: Him, Allah!

I am annihilated in Him and by Him,
He sees me just as I do Him.

None can take His place
Lovers have lost themselves in Him

Inebriated and amazed in Him
They reveal and speak about Him

He is my goal, that is no mystery.
My heart never forgets Him.

At times He dissolves me in Him,
And through me He emerges with His full splendor

Other times He perpetuates me through Him
"I" says I, then, not "He."

He! He! My desire is in Him,
My essence and my spirit love Him with passion.

Allah! Allah! I mention none other than Him,
All my words are His Glory.

My Beloved! My Beloved! I conceal Him
For I fear the day I meet Him…

He is my secret! I will not give Him away
Except to him who knows what He is.

He is my destination, for whom I forsake all things
He took my mind away from all that is not He!

It is by His Command that I speak
When I do it is by Him and for Him

I send a prayer that pleases Him
To the one He has favored and chosen

To his family and heirs,
And the ones who seek refuge in him

Al-Alawi is annihilated in Him,
He only desires His bliss

Muhammad, I know what is in him—
He contains all beauty.

O Lord, bless him,
A blessing worthy of his essence!

My Eyes Were Overwhelmed

My eyes were overwhelmed
The day He clearly revealed Himself.
The irresistible force of my Beloved
Is enough for me as an excuse—
A disturbance that dazzles the minds
I came to know Him when He appeared in me.

Thank God for that which my eye has seen.

It is a hidden secret disabling all but me,
Many are His Aspects! Who could know
That He can reveal Himself
As the heat of the embers?
Glory to Allah! He is no longer hidden from me!

Thank God for that which my eye has seen.

The spirit evolves in His Holy Presence
If only you could see, my friend,
What is behind the garb:
It is like a lamp in the niche of the sensible world,
Its inner meaning expresses itself in all forms.

Thank God for that which my eye has seen.

I declared my love out loud, I spread it among people.
I said: O noble ones
The beloved One, I have found Him!
Yet all men are deeply asleep
There are none to say he has seen Him
By God I swear He is never out of sight!

Thank God for that which my eye has seen.

All words are vain
Except those of the Beloved One.
It is impossible that they are not in existence.
All things are illusion, annihilated by realization
Except the Face of Allah, and that
Suffices him who has Vision

Thank God for that which my eye has seen.

O you who have eyes, if you are not that dazzled,
Ask yourself and contemplate:
Who then manifests himself through creation?
If you answer: Allah the All-Knowing
We will tell you: Conceal this secret
And that which you hear as coming from me,
Know that it is from Allah Himself.

Thank God for that which my eye has seen.

Truly I possess wisdom, in this art I am gifted
Eternally unique, I have no equal among people
I care not about the detractor who is unable
to grasp Him
Unmindful of God,
My art is beyond him.

Thank God for that which my eye has seen.

If only he could wake up from the torpor
Of the world of the senses
And take a companion towards the Holy Presence,

Like me, trustworthy, in the Station of Intimacy
By being sincere for Allah,
He would perceive my words.

Thank God for that which my eye has seen.

Certainly among the sciences,
There are proofs
That I am unique in this sublime station!
Know, O disciple, my name, and speak and guide,
Ben Aliwa has greater power than you.

Thank God for that which my eye has seen.

Wise Sayings

He who contemplates God through creatures
Loses sight of them by disappearing in Him
And there remains naught but the Divine.

The knowledge of Unity is like fire—
It enflames everything it comes upon,
And by this very act purifies it.

Do not forsake your soul (*nafs*), nor be its enemy—
Be its companion instead and try to search
What it holds within.

There is not a single atom in the universe that
Carries not in it one of the Names of the One Adored.

Notes

1. The direction towards Mecca to which all Muslims pray.
2. The self, the ego, the "carnal soul."
3. Wine mentioned in The Quran (XLVII: 15). By "wine" and "drink," the Sufis mean to taste of the divine Love.
4. Taha: a name of the Prophet.
5. The Pen.
6. Abul Qassem: a name of the Prophet.
7. Ben Aliwa: a name of the Shaykh al-Alawi.

Acre is a historic walled port-city with continuous settlement from the Phoenician period. The present-day city is characteristic of a fortified town dating from the Ottoman eighteenth and nineteenth centuries, with typical urban components such as the citadel, mosques, khans, and baths. The remains of the crusader town, dating from 1104 to 1291, lie almost intact, both above and below today's street level.

Selections from the Works of Fatima al-Yashrutiyya

In the Name of God, the Merciful, the Compassionate

My father and master, the divine Pole[1] of the age, heir to the essence of the Muhammadan legacy, our lord and master Shaykh Ali Nur al-Din al-Yashruti, al-Hasani by descent and origin, al-Shadhili by allegiance to that *ṭarīqa* and school of thought, al-Tunisi al-Maghribi by birth and upbringing, was born in the year 1791 in the city of Banzart (Bizerta) near Tunis. He left this world to meet his Lord in the year 1899 in Acre, Palestine, and was buried in his *zāwiya* there. To this day streams of visitors from all parts of the Islamic world make pilgrimages to his tomb. He (may God be pleased with him!) is descended from a long line of noble and dignified families, whose lineage goes back to the Messenger of God (peace and blessings be upon him!). His father was Muhammad ibn Nur al-Din al-Yashruti al-Hasani, one of the leading members of the Yashrut family, and a notable of Banzart. An upright, pious, God-fearing man with a strong personality, he was highly learned in Islamic studies. His mother was Sayyida Maryam Tajiriyya, of a family in Tunis. God granted her many sons and daughters, but three of them died in infancy, and another four only lived until adolescence, when they were stricken with plague and died within a week.

She was overcome by this tragedy and would have died from grief, had not God, by His mercy, given her a consolation and ordained that she bear our great Shaykh. With the coming of this dear child God took the parents' sadness away and restored to them their lost happiness. His birth had been foretold to his mother by a Sufi—a pious, saintly man from Morocco who once visited her and said, "God will bestow upon you an exceptional son, whose date of birth is in a verse of the Holy Quran." He told her this years before she bore him. And my father, while speaking to some of his companions in Acre about his mother, mentioned another instance when she was given tidings of his birth: "She (may God have mercy on her!) was beloved of the Sufis, and after all her children died she withdrew from the world and devoted herself to God, going at times to visit the graves of her children. One day, when she had just returned from one of these visits, Shaykh Muhammad Jallul, a Sufi saint of Banzart, knocked on the door. Upon entering he greeted her and said: 'O Maryam, you will carry in your womb and give birth to a son who you will name Ali Nur al-Din.' He then held out his hand and gave her a small stone, saying, 'Keep this, and when the boy attains manhood give it to him as a gift from me, and convey my greetings to him.' Then he departed."

Now my grandmother had not been acquainted with Shaykh Muhammad Jallul before, and had never gone to visit him, while he for his part, did not visit anyone at all, on account of the great number of people who were constantly asking to see him. For this reason my grandmother believed that this was a spiritual meeting and true prediction, and that Shaykh Muhammad Jallul had been inspired by God. Her soul was filled with peace and serenity and she regained hope after her time of suffering.

Among the graces bestowed upon my father and perfect guide (may God sanctify his secret!), was that he was raised in an ambiance of piety and was given a religious education. His parents were energetic and highly intelligent, and although there were no spiritual masters in either family, those who were theologians were learned in "outer" knowledge, and many of them were officials and judges. God showed his favor to my father (may He be pleased with him!) and raised him to the station of His worship even as a young child. He made him submissive to Him through obedience to his parents in what was pleasing to God and his Messenger. He thus conformed to the wisdom of the verse: "And lower to them the wing of submissiveness in mercy, and say, 'My Lord! Have mercy on them both, for they cared for me from birth.'"[2] He was a perfected man, characterized by compassion, mercy, and self-sacrifice; he loved all of God's creatures with a noble and detached love, which embraces everything, man, or animal.

Injustices committed by one human being to another grieved him, as did injustices by man to birds and animals. Whenever he saw a man being cruel to his animal he would plead with him to show mercy to the helpless creature, and if he saw a bird in a cage he would set it free. He used to walk in the streets where small birds are sold for children to play with, in order to buy them and let them go, watching their soaring flight to freedom. He was a true servant of God. He took action according to His order or His forbidding, and for this He filled him with his grace and raised him above others around him, protecting him from the darkness of the created world and granting him the grace of His nearness. It is no wonder then, that he did not seek the company of the doctors of the law at any stage of his life, nor did he even visit them, regardless of who they were. Instead, he devoted himself to the service of Sufi disciples and those who were in need. His fervent love for the people of God had existed since he was very young, for he had never occupied himself with things of a worldly nature. He had many interesting encounters with them, and although space does not permit us to recount them all here, the following is one example: He would often go to a mosque in which there lived a pious, saintly man whom he loved. One day in the evening he went to this mosque to take the man some food. When he arrived some time had passed since the evening prayer, and he found him standing in his room at the mosque absorbed in devotion and prayer. My father stopped and waited at the door, but no sooner had he finished his prayer, than he began to practice the invocation of God without turning around and did not see my father. The two remained thus until dawn—my father standing, the fear of God in him—and the Sufi completely immersed in the state of remembrance of God. When the call to prayer was made at dawn, the Sufi stood up and turned, and saw, to his astonishment, my father still standing in his place, filled with awe. He approached him and asked, "When did you come here, Ali?" "In the evening," he answered. "And how is it you are still standing there?" My father bowed his head in silence, and at that the man raised his hands in supplication and prayed for him. Then he asked him why he had come and what he wanted, and my father said, "I would like you to give me advice that will help me in my religion." The Sufi said: "Befriend no one but the truthful." "Everyone lays claim to truthfulness," my father said. The Sufi replied: "I will give you the criterion whereby you shall know the truthful from those who speak falsehoods: Whoever leads you towards God is truthful, and whoever leads you towards this world speaks falsehoods."

My father (may God be pleased with him!) pursued his studies in Banzart and Tunis. He was a shining pinnacle of learning and an example by his deeds and pious fear of God, for he was foremost in worship, fasting, keeping vigil at night, and in practicing remembrance of God. This had always been his way, for he (may God be pleased with him!)

was a Sufi by nature, illuminated by the light of divine knowledge and certitude. He was of those whom God favored according to the wisdom of the noble verse: "And when they listen to that which was revealed to the Messenger, thou seest their eyes overflowing with tears because of their recognition of the Truth."[3] He had realized that he could achieve the "clear victory"[4] over the world only at the hand of a perfected guide, one who was a realized sage, and who was the spiritual Pole of the age. He was always searching for this guide, and had met and sat in the circles of many theologians and doctors of the law, as well as Shaykhs and men of God. Whenever he heard of a great teacher or of a Shaykh with much wisdom, he would invariably make straight for that person and attach himself to him, and he was received into several Sufi *ṭarīqas* in this way. When he had attained the station of the Shaykh of a *ṭarīqa* he would request of him that he bestow more graces upon him, whereupon the Shaykh would reply: "I possess no more than what you have already attained to." At this my father would take his leave of him and go in search of another master. Now among the *ṭarīqas* that he was associated with was that of Shaykh ibn Isa.[5] After spending some months there reciting the litanies of the order, he saw Shaykh ibn Isa in a vision. My father approached him and said: "I have recited the litanies, but have not yet been rewarded through them." Shaykh ibn Isa said: "You are a good man, Ali. What are you in need of?" He replied, "If you have any higher knowledge, aid me by teaching it to me." The Shaykh said, "You know well I am in the isthmus (*barzakh*) between the saints and those who have only indirect knowledge, and do not possess anything myself, but I will guide you to one who will give you the secret which the Prophet (peace and blessings be upon him!) gave to Ali ibn Abi Talib (may God honor his countenance!)."[6] My father awoke in the morning joyful on account of the vision he had had, and several days later the Shaykh's name was mentioned to him—it was our lord and master Shaykh Muhammad ibn Hamza Zafir al-Madani (may God sanctify his secret!) My father determined to travel to Misuratah[7] for the sake of God and His Messenger—"And whosoever emigrates for God and His Messenger, his emigration is for God and His Messenger."[8] "Glory be to Him who has not made a sign leading to His saints except as a sign leading to Himself, and has caused no one to attach himself to them except he whom He wishes to attach to Himself."[9]

Before presenting himself before his Shaykh, my father divested himself of all his former knowledge and works. He thus appeared before his master in perfect humility, stripped of all acquisitions. His Shaykh met him and greeted him warmly, and after returning his greeting, and making supplication to God, my father sat before his Shaykh and requested to be accepted to the Madani Shadhili *ṭarīqa* and to serve him as his disciple. He then added, "If I am granted anything from you, then this is by the Grace of God; and if not, then I will take what I can from you to obtain your blessings." His Shaykh said, "Welcome to you, O Ali. Glory be to God! Are you not then content with the vision you had some days ago?" He then initiated him into the Madani Shadhili *ṭarīqa*, and ordered him to invoke the Supreme Name and to practice the remembrance of God secretly and openly. He gave him permission to recite the litanies of the *ṭarīqa* and to initiate into the path whomever was suited for it. In this way he made him a representative to the *fuqarāʾ*[10], and thus his victory over the lower world began.

God, powerful and majestic, raised my father and master (may God be pleased with him!) to the level of seclusion (*tajrīd*) since the time he began to shun the created world and incline towards the truth. Then, when he reached the flower of youth, his Lord made him completely devoted to Himself, and placed him before his great Shaykh, and under his protection—he was a *faqīr* renouncing the world, in a house wherein the Name of God is invoked much. The Most High said in His mighty Book: "… in houses which God hath allowed to be exalted and that His Name shall be remembered therein. Therein offer praise to Him at morning and evening, men whom neither merchandise nor sale beguileth from the remembrance of God, and consistency in prayer and paying to the poor their due; who fear a day when hearts and eyes will be overturned; that God may reward them with the best of what they did and increase reward for them of His Bounty. Verily, God giveth sustenance without measure to whom He will."[11]

Those who follow the path of knowledge, and wish to unite with God most high, travel to him as a lightning bolt, without turning towards what emanates from Him of phenomena, nor fearing that which they are approaching. The lights of guidance are only needed for those on the path. As for those who are united to God, theirs are the lights of union; for they did not follow secondary lights, but rather penetrated to the Light of lights. It is because of this that they became the Sufi masters—one is the *murīd*, and the other the *murād*.[12]

My honored father (may God be pleased with him!) remained isolated from the world for thirteen years near his master in the *zāwiya* at Misuratah. He lived under the banner of his Shaykh's love, listening to his wise counsels, which were without number. He beheld his great knowledge and enlightenment, his attributes and his graces, and all of this made my father extinguish himself in his Shaykh.

He thus became endowed with his characteristics, was united with his Muhammadan qualities, received from him his knowledge and wisdom, and was perfected through his Shaykh's perfection. He was of those chosen by God and his Shaykh was aware of God's will in this; he knew that this spiritual son was the inheritor of the Prophet's legacy after him, and so he drew him near to him and chose him above others as his closest disciple, disclosing to him of his great knowledge from the ocean of realities and wisdom.

After he was permitted by his Shaykh to initiate others into the *ṭarīqa*, to explain matters to disciples, and to show them the way to perfection, he began to travel by order of his master from one place to another, going to cities, villages, and desert tribes to teach the disciples about their religion and to inspire them to practice the remembrance of God. He would only accept those into the *ṭarīqa* whom he deemed fit—those who were sincere and patient in the face of the vicissitudes of life. He never traveled beyond North Africa until his Shaykh passed away and after his mother's death.

My father had never had to work in the world, even in his youth, because his father had left him a source of income from the profits of his properties and farmland, and this was sufficient for him to live and to spend in addition a good deal in the way of God and His Messenger. From time to time during his period of isolation at the *zāwiya* he would ask permission of his Shaykh to go and visit his mother and relatives in Banzart for a period of time. Although many people think that isolation (*tajrīd*) is the same as monasticism, it is clearly different from it. The following are words of our Shaykh Abu al-Hasan[13] (may God be pleased with him!): "This Path has nothing to do with monasticism or the eating of bran and barley, etc." The disciple may marry while in isolation, or he may enter into isolation while married. He may remain thus for several years, and then God, mighty and powerful, may ordain that he have an occupation in the world. The will of the Sufi disciple is submitted to the will of God for him. My father had married in his home in Banzart during the period of his isolation in the *zāwiya* in Misuratah, and he used to go from time to time to visit his mother and family, but he never stayed very long before returning to the sacred ambiance of the Shadhili in Misuratah.

The era of spiritual guidance through the Muhammadan legacy began in my father's life after the departure of his Shaykh to the eternal abode. It was then that his extraordinary spiritual station manifested itself. At the time his Shaykh passed away my father was not in the *zāwiya* but on one of his journeys in the Maghrib[14] exhorting men to follow the way to God. When the news of his Shaykh's death reached him, he was full of grief, and lacking the strength to continue his work, he returned to his master's *zāwiya* to take up any duties the departed one or his honored children had for him. He remained there only a few days, however, and then returned to his region having been given the Muhammadan legacy by God and began to call people to the path, initiating those who were qualified for it into the Shadhili *ṭarīqa*. He then resolved to undertake a journey that was destined to be filled with blessings, and was to extend over many years. Now, in those days travel was fraught with dangers from land and sea, whether traveling by boat, by camel and donkey, or on foot. Even so he set off accompanied by nine other men from the Maghrib, going from place to place through Africa and Asia. He suffered hunger and thirst at times and was forced to travel through violent sandstorms while observing the fast of the month of Ramadan. He encountered primitive, savage tribes, but God aided him and supported him by His Spirit so that all his meetings ended by guiding many to the path. During his travels he made it a practice to stay several days to a few weeks in one place, but never as much as a full month. He never ordered the disciples who came to him to leave their professions, and exhorted them to view the rest of mankind with their different religious beliefs with tolerance and kindness.

After my father had spent ten years in the service of Islam and Muslims, an inspiration came to him from our most wise Lord to perform the pilgrimage to Mecca. So he set off towards the Hijaz with his companions and lived there for four years next to the tomb of the Prophet, and made the pilgrimage every year. After this stay in the Hijaz he decided to visit the tomb of our greatest Shaykh, after whom the Shadhili *ṭarīqa* is named—our master Ali abu al-Hasan al-Shadhili (may God sanctify his secret!). His tomb is visited by many to this day and is located in Egypt near the coast of the Red Sea. Following this sacred visit, he was moved by the divine Will to make a journey to Syria in order to visit the Aqsa mosque in Jerusalem. He went to Alexandria and embarked on a boat there that was going to Jaffa. By the will and power of God, they were caught in a terrible storm while at sea; the boat was unable to set shore at Jaffa, and instead was cast ashore between the cities of Beirut and Sidon, near to the tomb of the prophet Jonah (upon him be peace!). Now the captain and owner of this boat was from Beirut, and was a pious man who loved the people of God. He had refused to take payment from my father and his two companions, so at this time my father said, "Hold out your hand, I wish to repay you," and he initiated him into the Shadhili *ṭarīqa*. He was thus the first man from this country to enter the *ṭarīqa* with our Shaykh, and he became one of his most sincere followers. My father then went ashore and spent his first night in Syria next to the tomb of the prophet Jonah. This prophet welcomed him into his holy sanctuary, greeted him, and encouraged him, saying, "O Ali! Establish your struggle for the sake of God in Acre." The prophet embraced him and prayed for him to be given a clear victory and triumph. My father perceived the presence of this noble prophet in a waking vision, and not as a dream. Thus, the following morning he set off towards Acre on foot, and from the moment he caught sight of the town, standing next to the tomb of the prophet Salih, (peace and blessings be upon him!) outside the wall of the city, he understood the destiny which God Most High had decreed for him. He knew that here was to be his abode, here was to be the dawn of the lights of truth and sanctity. God had granted him a spiritual home, and the spirit which used to compel him to pursue his travels from one place to another had now ceased to do so, after wandering for fourteen years, calling men to God and striving for Him in the sacred journey to God and His Messenger.

The Ottoman Empire ruled over Syria then, its boundaries touching Egypt in the south, and Iraq in the east, for what was then called Syria (*al-shām*) encompassed present day Lebanon, Syria, Palestine, and East Jordan. The city of Acre was a fortressed stronghold with a long history of wars, sieges, and enemy blockades. There were two gates to the city, one from the east towards land and the other facing the sea. Behind the walls was a deep, wide trench with passageways over it. The sea lay on three sides of the city, and extending beyond the walls and trench to the east was a plain of green, fertile fields where fragrant flowers, herbs, and lilies bloomed in the spring. In those days the authorities did not permit people to plant trees on the borders of the fields, nor to erect any buildings because it was an important military stronghold and the army had complete control of it. Thus was Acre when my father arrived there in 1849.

Our master entered the city and went to the Zaytuna mosque, where many people were gathered for prayer. Now scarcely had he sat down after the prayer and begun to speak with the wisdom, subtle knowledge, and illumination with which God filled him, when people gathered around him to listen. They were astonished by what they heard and drew closer, for his utterances were those of one chosen by God to guide the aspirant. His station (may God be pleased with him!) was such that his heart was silent in the presence of God, mighty and powerful, and could hear within itself the echoes of divine knowledge and realization. It was inevitable that men of intelligence would respond to his message, and that the hearts of those from east and west would be attracted to him, for whosoever submits to God has all his creatures submitted to him in turn.

The Sufi does not content himself with the outward acts of worship prescribed by religion, but perceives by God's light the wisdom and essence concealed within dogmas and forms, and strives to extract these secrets from their hidden depths. In this way he comes to realize the essence of prayer. He does not pray with his thoughts wandering and his heart distracted, for by giving himself up to prayer and to the remembrance of God he is carried from his own forgetfulness to God's presence, and from His presence to the unveiling of that which is hidden, until he becomes extinguished in the One invoked. He who prays should be absorbed in remembrance during prayer. The Most High has said: "Verily prayer guards against vile and loathsome deeds, but verily the remembrance of God is of all things the greatest."[15] And the Shaykh al-Akbar, Sidi Muhy al-Din ibn Arabi (may God be pleased with him!) said: "Remembrance of God is greater than all words and deeds." It encompasses all worship, being an interior discourse between the servant and his Lord. For this reason, the disciple in prayer must cease from dwelling in outwardness and withdraw into the heart, thus cutting himself off from anything apart from God. He will then behold the greatness of the One invoked by the Name of Majesty "as though he were seeing Him."[16]

Some of the notables of the city offered to serve my father themselves, while others sent their young sons and daughters to serve him. However, on account of his poor health, his doctor decided he must move to the mountains. He could either go to the village of Safad, or to Tarshiha. The latter was close to Acre, so our master chose to go there, still accompanied by two of his companions from the Maghrib who never parted with him until their deaths in this country.[17] One was buried in Tarshiha and the other in Acre, near the tomb of the prophet Salih. After he had settled into his spiritual home, content and favored by God, the *ṭarīqa* began to spread gradually to Acre, Safad, Jerusalem, Damascus, Aleppo, Tripoli, Beirut, Sidon, Haifa, Jaffa, and elsewhere. Now because of the great number of visitors coming to Tarshiha, some enemies of God spread false rumors about my father (may God be pleased with him!) saying that he had established a fortified stronghold in the mountains, and had hidden there one hundred thousand soldiers, fully armed, with the intention of leading a revolt against the Ottoman state. On hearing this rumor the government became concerned, and this concern soon turned into anxiety for its safety. A revolt by some citizens of

Acre had been attempted not long before, and prior to that there had been a siege upon the city. They thus ordered my father into exile to the island of Rhodes. A ship was sent from Istanbul carrying military officials and soldiers to convey our Shaykh to his destination and to surround the *zāwiya* in case of trouble when the Shaykh was taken away, or so they imagined might occur. The same day the boat arrived at Beirut, the army set off by land, traveling over the mountains, and reaching Tarshiha, surrounding the *zāwiya*. However, the commander could find nothing there of which the rumors had claimed—neither stronghold nor army, and he regretted his deed, for instead he saw before him a modest house with special rooms in it for performing religious rites, and he saw many of the disciples—men of piety and virtue, extinguished in their love of God and His Messenger. They were those whose "faces are marked with the traces of prostration."[18] He walked into the house, feeling very embarrassed, and meeting my father (may God be pleased with him!), he kissed both his hands, asked his pardon for the misunderstanding, and beseeched forgiveness from God. Then he told him, "I am a mere servant bound by my orders, and am powerless to change them." My father, responding with the kindness and great humility for which he was known, gave him his blessings. They then took him away, informing no one of their destination; nor did my father ask where they were leading him.

After living for twenty-one months in Rhodes, the Ottoman government realized its mistake and apologized to my father. They offered to provide a monthly stipend of ten gold dinars for the *zāwiya* he had established in Rhodes and offered him the position of Shaykh to the sultan in Istanbul. He refused this position and asked instead to return to Tarshiha. The government, however, would not grant him permission to return and live there on a permanent basis, but rather gave him the freedom to choose any other place to live. And so after returning to Tarshiha, and being welcomed by joyful brethren, loved ones and friends, he decided that his permanent place of residence should be in Acre. He was welcomed on his arrival there by his disciples with much joy and celebration, and his return to that city was a source of blessings for all its inhabitants.

The *Zāwiya* and its Surroundings

The *zāwiya* is a place where religious rites are performed; it is a place for prayer, fasting, night vigil, reflection, invocation, meditation, and total concentration on God. It is there that the litanies are recited, circles of *dhikr* (invocation) are held, and the *faqīr* cuts himself off from anything other than God, the glorious. It is there that knowledge and realization are sought, where union with God, mighty and majestic, is witnessed and realized, and where the disciple is extinguished in love of God and His Messenger.

The *takīya* is the great sanctuary, with a high dome, in which the five prayers and sessions of *dhikr* are held. There are in addition many rooms in the *zāwiya* to house visitors during their stay and for those disciples who are in isolation from the world. Then there are small houses in which the families of those in isolation live; there are special sections for the old and sick, for the poor followers of the path, and one set apart for women. The Shaykh's house was in the vicinity of the *zāwiya* where he lived with his wife and children. The greatness of the *zāwiya* was due, not to the beauty and grandeur of its outward appearance, but to the great saintliness of its Shaykh and his divine station, for he was filled by God with mystical secrets and lights, and with knowledge and understanding. This was how our *zāwiya* was in my honored father's time; the spiritual life there was sweet with worship, remembrance, mysteries, and divine illuminations. Winds of grace and holiness swept through the realms of religious learning, both outward and inward, during the meeting of *dhikr*, in lessons of literature and the arts, during meditation and in singing spiritual songs. This holy breeze wafted throughout the atmosphere of the Sufi, for although Islamic learning has many aspects, it is in essence a spiritual education that can be reduced to the acts of worship and remembrance of God.

Every evening, study circles were held in our *zāwiya* where lessons of Islamic Law, *ḥadīth*, Quranic commentary, and Sufism were read as well as other aspects of the sciences of the outer law and inner truth. In those days the *zāwiya* resembled an institute of learning that was attended by various groups of people not only for the purpose of following a spiritual path and seeking enlightenment, but also to benefit from that sacred spring of wisdom, each one to the extent of his desire and need for religious education and spiritual direction. The sessions of *dhikr* were attended by adherents of both exoteric and esoteric knowledge. They included men of authority, the rich and the poor; and it sometimes happened that a person could not find a place to sit in that great sanctuary on account of the multitude of people who used to come to listen to our Shaykh. My honored father performed the five daily prayers in the *takīya* along with his representatives (*muqaddams*), elder disciples, visitors, disciples in isolation, and those living nearby, who also came to pray with him. The great numbers of visitors to the *zāwiya* filled one with awe and reverence; the rows of men at prayer were often so numerous that they even overflowed into the outer hallways of the mosque.

Holding circles of *dhikr* in which the testimony of faith (*lā ilāha illa Allāh*)[19] is recited is permitted by religious law, and the right of the believer to invoke is mentioned clearly in several places in the Quran, among them the following: "Remember God with much remembrance, and glorify Him morning and evening."[20] And His words: "Those who remember God standing, sitting, and lying on their sides."[21] And: "Is it not in the remembrance of God that hearts find peace?"[22] There are also many *ḥadīths* that speak of the right to invoke and to hold circles of *dhikr*. Of these, the following was transmitted by Tirmidhi. He said: "The Messenger of God said: 'Whenever you pass by the meadows of Paradise, graze therein.' They asked, 'O Messenger of God, what are the meadows of Paradise?' He replied, 'The circles of *dhikr*.'"[23] Badhdhar transmitted on the authority of Anas (may God be pleased with him!) that the Prophet (peace and blessings be upon him!) said: "Verily God has angels who travel about seeking out the circles of *dhikr*, and whenever they come upon one, they surround it and God says to them, 'Enfold them in My mercy, for they are of those who sit together (to invoke) and whose sitting thus will not cause them sorrow.'"

The Disciple

The Sufi disciple who is attached to God's path could be in isolation from the world, or working and earning his living as others. The one in isolation must cut himself off from what is apart from God, and devote himself completely to Him. The second type, for his part, enters the path while continuing in his outward life, working to earn his living and performing his worldly duties. In this respect, the disciples are divided into two groups, yet they are all united in a common path under the direction of a realized Shaykh who has been given the function to guide. For the aspirant who follows a spiritual path under a perfected Shaykh, all of his experiences and states exist only as a reflection of those of his master, and by means of him. This is what is meant when it is said that extinction (*fanāʾ*) is divided into three stages: The first is in the Shaykh, the second in the Muhammadan essence, and the third is in God, mighty and exalted. The attainment of the second level of extinction should not sever the fundamental link between the disciple and his Shaykh, for the successful and joyful disciple is he who never forgets his master, regardless of his spiritual state or station.

Those who work in the world are divided into three subcategories: first, those who earn their livelihood in their own countries, come to visit their Shaykh and return home again; second, those who work and live in the town near the *zāwiya*; and third, those who emigrate from their country in order to be near their Shaykh or to find work for themselves in the nearby town.

Those who have been placed by their Lord, glorified and most high, in the station of isolation from the world live in the *zāwiya* near the master, and having devoted themselves to God in this way, they no longer turn towards the world. There was a great number of these disciples in our *zāwiya*—men who came from all manner of social class and ethnic origin. Among them were Arabs, Turks, Moroccans, Indians, Persians, and Sudanese. These disciples were outwardly and inwardly brethren in God; men who conformed to the Muhammadan norm in order to purify their souls and polish their characters, to efface their lower selves and become immersed in the consciousness of the essence of God most high.

It is the duty of everyone attached to the Yashruti Shadhili *ṭarīqa* to recite its litanies every morning and evening after the dawn and sunset prayers. This consists of saying the following: "I ask forgiveness of God, the mighty, than whom there is no other god, the living, the eternal, and I turn in repentance to Him."[24] This is recited one hundred times, followed by the prayer on the Prophet, his family, and companions one hundred times, and then the words "there is no divinity but God"[25] one hundred times, ending with the words, "Muhammad is the Messenger of God, peace and blessings be upon him!" Of asking forgiveness of God in the first part of the litany, the Quran says, "Seek forgiveness of your Lord. Verily, He is ever forgiving. He will let loose the sky for you in abundant rain, and will help you with wealth and sons, and will assign unto you gardens and will assign unto you rivers."[26] And our Shaykh Abu al-Hasan al-Shadhili said, "It is incumbent upon you to ask forgiveness of God, even if there be no sin; consider the Prophet's practice of asking forgiveness, even after being given glad tidings and the certitude of forgiveness for his former sins and those he was to commit. Here is someone infallible, who had never committed a sin, and who was holy. What, then, would you think of someone who was guilty from time to time of sin and wrongdoing?"[27] The prayer on the Prophet is performed in accordance with the verse: "Verily God and His angels bless the Prophet. O ye who believe, bless him and salute him with a worthy salutation."[28] Shaykh Mustafa Naja, mufti of Beirut said of this verse, "... the Doctors of the Law are agreed that this noble verse shows the greatness and power of the Prophet (peace and blessings be upon him!) above all others."[29] Regarding the formula of the unity of God, Imam Ahmad, Tabarani, and others related that the Prophet used to teach his companions in groups and singly. Concerning their group teachings, Shaddad ibn Aus related, "We were with the Prophet, and he asked us, 'Is there a stranger among you?'—meaning of the People of the Book[30]—and we replied, 'No, O Messenger of God.' He then ordered that the door be locked, and said, 'Raise your hands and say, "There is no divinity but God."' So we raised our hands and said it. Then he said, 'Praise be to God—O God, you have sent me with this word and given me orders concerning it, and promised me Paradise because of it. Verily you will not put off the Appointed Time.' Then he said, 'Give glad tidings, for God has forgiven you.'"[31] Concerning his teaching to his companions singly, Shaykh Yusuf al-Kurani al-Ajami related the following *ḥadīth*: "Ali asked the Prophet: 'O Messenger of God, show me the path which will bring me nearest to you, that which is easiest for the worshipper to follow and is the most pleasing to God.' He replied, 'The best of what I and the Prophets before me have said is "there is no divinity save God." And even if the seven heavens and the seven earths were in one scale, and "there is no divinity save God" were in another scale, "there is no divinity save God" would be of greater weight.'"[32]

Advancement on the path of the Sufi masters is not obtained by holding circles of *dhikr* openly, for this is something everyone owes to God. Rather, it is obtained by practicing the remembrance of God in secret through repeating the Supreme Name *Allāh*. This is the second pillar of the Shadhili masters' path, the first being the existence of a realized and perfected sage, for without him the *dhākir* (one who practices remembrance) would not be able to attain to the peace and fulfillment contained in the invocation. The *faqīr* who wishes to practice the invocation should choose a peaceful, quiet place, during the night or the day, but more often at night, where he can sit to remember God, either with knees drawn up as a sign of humility, or cross legged and in both cases wrapped in a cloak. It was related that the

Prophet (peace and blessings be upon him!) used to sit with knees drawn up, holding a garment wrapped around him.[33] This name is the Supreme Name which the aspirant invokes and without which no victory will come to him, nor will he attain to the station of the saintly save by invoking It. Moreover, he cannot truly invoke unless he cuts himself off from everything other than the One Invoked, for the Shadhili *ṭarīqa* is founded on the holy Book and the practices of the Prophet, the search for knowledge, and the frequent practice of the invocation in an attitude of worship and consciousness of the divine. Now this means of calling upon God is the easiest and most direct of paths, for it does not entail great hardships or much strenuous effort. The primordial light lying dormant within the soul gains strength by the light of knowledge and by the light of the invocation, so that the soul is rid of its defects and impurities and can then draw ever nearer to the divine presence until it is completely absorbed in it and the invocation burns away all thoughts of anything other than the Invoked.

People are often heard to say that the disciples of Sufi dwellings live a life of indolence and ease, but in our *zāwiya* they were not thus. Each disciple had duties that he performed to the best of his ability, depending on his preparation and education. These duties were not a burden for him, but were part of life in the *zāwiya* and were done in an attitude of friendship and affection towards others. All of the disciples were equal before God; the wise and learned taught the illiterate and the common man, striving to teach him the doctrinal knowledge that makes the Muhammadan initiation accessible to him. The great dealt gently with the weak, and the elevated man gave guidance to his humbler brother.

The Shaykh appoints a representative in the *zāwiya*, who is authorized to initiate others into the *ṭarīqa*, to educate disciples, to lead the sessions of *dhikr*, and to teach religious studies. This representative must be someone who is well educated and eloquent, possessed of an excellent character, and endowed with wisdom and understanding. He must combine in his person knowledge of both legal and spiritual matters. He could be chosen either from those in isolation or from those working in the world, for neither one is more worthy than the other for this position.

Concern for health and cleanliness was of the greatest importance in our *zāwiya*, indeed to a degree that surpasses description. If my honored father fell ill, the doctor was summoned immediately, and thus it was with his wife and family or any of his disciples. If someone needed to be under a doctor's supervision he was sent to the hospital in Acre. If he had to undergo surgery in one of the bigger hospitals in Beirut, there he was sent. If he needed a change of climate he went to the mountains, and whenever someone was afflicted with an infectious disease he was isolated from the rest of the disciples. Thus it was that in spite of the great numbers of visitors, nomads or settled folk, the concern for health and cleanliness was at the forefront. In reality life in our *zāwiya* was not like the life of dervishes, but was a life of spiritual progress combining invocation, learning, worship, and realization. Through carrying out our human duties and diligently striving through the levels of perfection—and by this last I mean the spiritual stations—one could arrive at the station of proximity (*qurb*) to God most high.

Our *zāwiya* offered food to visiting disciples, and we often had no less than four or five hundred every day, apart from those living there in isolation with their wives and children. These visitors stayed in the *zāwiya* and at mealtimes the tablecloths were laid and the disciples sat in groups to eat, while some helped to serve, carrying jugs of water and singing spiritual songs. During the feast days the number of visitors could reach between one and two thousand each day.

Whatever money accrued from religious charities was spent on the *zāwiya*, as well as any other money and gifts the disciples offered to it; the Shaykh's money, when he had any, was also spent on the *zāwiya* and thus everyone participated in its upkeep. If the *zāwiya* happened to own some farmland or olive groves and the like, those who were farmers in retreat would set about cultivating it, tilling it, gathering the harvest, picking the fruits, and putting the olives in a press to extract the oil. They worked at transporting the provisions, and in raising livestock. Some also worked at weaving clothing, combing the cotton from the beds, buying necessities from the market, sweeping, cleaning, polishing, and whatever else was necessary for the maintenance of the *zāwiya*.

The majority of those in retreat in our *zāwiya* in my father's time were of noble and very old families. My father used to exhort them to give their whole heart and to extinguish themselves in the love of God and His Messenger. He treated them as a father would his children, never differentiating between them and my brother Sidi Muhy al-Din—in fact he often said, "If Muhy al-Din were not a disciple, I would not be disposed to love him." My brother Sidi Ibrahim came from Tunis, bringing his wife and children after the death of his brother Muhy al-Din. Now our master had no male children other than he, and in spite of this, he ordered him to follow the path as one in isolation from the world for some years along with the other disciples before coming to live in his father's house. He slept with the disciples and assisted them by helping to construct buildings, carrying clay with his hands and wearing dyed linen garments. My sister's son Sidi Hasan led the same life. Our brother in God Sidi Mahmud al-Lahham related according to his brother Sidi Abd Allah—sons of the great Shaykh Muhy al-Din al-Lahham—the following: "We were in the *zāwiya* and heard news of the arrival of Sidi Ibrahim, son of our great master, in Haifa. I was with a group of our disciples from Damascus, and we all decided to go to Haifa and take the rest of the disciples in the *zāwiya* to welcome him. Now our Shaykh was nearby and when he saw our group he said, "Do not behave with him as the disciples of Shaykh So-and-so behave with his sons; they pamper and entertain them and dress them in silk. As a result the children start to walk about and look at themselves and become cut off from closeness to God." And so we remained in the *zāwiya*, and not even one of us went to welcome the Shaykh's son. He came with his family and entered into the *zāwiya* unaccompanied. My father also said to some disciples after my brother's arrival in Acre, "Leave him to be taught by the *ṭarīqa*."

Our Shaykh was ascetic in the true sense of the word; he avoided the things of this world in spite of the fact that he was always being offered them. If he was given something he would spend it in God's name. Our brother Shaykh Ibrahim al-Kanafani related to me: "It was the habit of our Shaykh whenever he went to the town to stop by the shop of one of our disciples of humble circumstance named Yusuf al-Safadi. Once a man from the city came into the shop when he was there and began to complain to him of his unfortunate state, requesting him to pray that his problems be solved for him, for he was in a difficult way financially and was in great distress. In the course of the conversation, a visiting disciple came in and presented some money to our Shaykh wrapped in a handkerchief. He took it, and without opening it placed it gently into the pocket of the bankrupt merchant, indicating by a sign to the others seated that they should make no remark about it. When the man went home he discovered fifty gold Ottoman dinars in the handkerchief. He returned to our Shaykh with news of what he had found, telling him he thought the sum very great. The Shaykh replied, 'It is for you to use to improve your circumstances.'"

The disciples were extinguished in their love for their master, and preferred the life of isolation to that of work in the world so they could be near him at all times. However, he did not order any of his disciples to leave their professions, businesses, or posts; the perfected one is he who moves among people while performing his duties. There is no work which God has made lawful that does not help the servant draw nearer to His presence; it only deters those who lack pure intentions in their work—whether it be in the field of learning, labor, or a professional career. A disciple once came to our master and asked permission to leave his work and give himself up completely to worship. The Shaykh said: "Remain in your shop and work and pray to your Lord; that is better for you than begging for food from people."

The disciples were proud and used to boast of having had visions of our noble Shaykh. They would compete with each other and believed that if his gaze merely fell upon a disciple he was transported to a higher state, and would attain realization. But the Shaykh himself knew that the divine light was not limited in this way and could come to the disciple anywhere, be he even at the ends of the earth. Many visited the Shaykh for the purpose of acquiring his qualities and characteristics which were an embodiment of the Muhammadan nature. When our brother Uthman Pasha, a Turkish minister in the Ottoman state, once visited him he said to our Shaykh: "I have been honored with a vision of our master; am I not then better than Ali Rida Pasha?" The Shaykh answered him by saying, "Being united to the essences is better than being united to the qualities." When Shaykh Hafiz Uthman, the famous Turkish reciter of the Quran came to visit my father, he had composed a poem during his journey at sea and when he entered the *zāwiya* my father asked about the poem he had composed, although no one had known anything about it. The Shaykh was astonished and asked, "Do you know what is hidden, or has a spirit inspired you?" Our Shaykh answered, "Do you not recite the noble Quran?" "Certainly," he said. "God has said in His mighty Book, 'The Knower of the unseen, which He revealeth unto none save every Messenger whom He hath chosen.'[34] I am of those the Messenger of God has chosen, for I am descended from him and linked to him." At this, Shaykh Uthman was filled with joy, entered into the Shadhili *ṭarīqa*, and was of those who attained to knowledge of God. The Shaykh also said to him while giving a talk one day, "You are of those who have preserved the Quran in memory. Our Lord, glorious and most high has favored us with you." Shaykh Uthman answered, "...with those who put the prescriptions into practice.'" Our Shaykh said, "Is there anyone aside from our Prophet who practices everything in the Quran? Rather, do you not practice part of it, even if only a single letter?" "Certainly," he said. The Shaykh replied, "This suffices." He also said, referring to the Sufi masters: "When you are told that there lives in Syria a great wise man, learned in the sciences of the outward and the inward and in gnosis and realization, one possessing pleasing qualities and Muhammadan characteristics, that which comes to you is the lore of certainty (*ᶜilm al-yaqīn*); and when you have abided with him and realized his outward and inward qualities, and found him to be above that which they described to you, your knowledge of him becomes the truth of certainty (*ḥaqq al-yaqīn*). Thus what is it that has disappeared between yourself and him, when neither he nor you have changed, and there has been no increase or decrease in his being or in yours? The answer is that what has disappeared is your ignorance of him."

He was once asked about smoking and the reason for its being something disliked in religion. He replied, "Smoking is a contradiction of the divine order, for God blessed and most high, has made man's life composed of two motions of breathing—inhaling and exhaling. The inhalation takes in pure cold air which contains life, and the exhalation comes out warm and soiled. When one smokes, he takes in warm air, and some of this finds its way to the lung passages. With time, it becomes dry and various diseases manifest themselves and become the cause of death by the will and judgment of God."

One day, speaking to a group of disciples, he said, "The eagle flies about in space, forming a circle with his wings like the circle of *dhikr*. Each time he ascends, he spreads out his wings and reposes, obtaining wisdom from Heaven. He continues thus until he reaches the highest station of wisdom, and then he reposes completely. God most high has said: 'And in the heavens is your sustenance and that which ye are promised.'[35] Now, do you know what causes this bird to descend in spite of this, from the highest station to the lowest? God glorious and most high has granted the eagle sharp vision; he sees the smallest of creatures on the earth while in the air, and it is desire for them which causes him to plunge down as low as this earth. Do you understand how this comes about? When the eagle is high up and spies a body on the ground he falls upon it, unconscious of all else and with such great determination that if he should strike a tree or a branch in his fall it would break his wing or take out his eye, or if he were to fall on a boulder his head would be crushed. The essence or inward meaning of this is that he is still bound by desire and his soul tends toward the material."

Sidi Mustafa al-Sadi was once reading from the Book of Unity (*tawḥīd*), and my father (may God be pleased with him!) asked him what the four founders of the schools of law had agreed upon concerning it. He answered, "There is no divinity save God." My father said, "That there is no divinity save God there can be no doubt or uncertainty, but only those who belong to *tawḥīd* may say, 'there is no divinity save God, Muhammad is the Messenger of God.'" And he asked Shaykh Ismail al-Tubasi, "What is your testimony about this?" Shaykh Ismail was silent and my father said, "There is naught in your testimony save God, is this not so?" "Of course," he replied. "The People of the Book say, 'There is naught in me save God'; and I say, 'There is no divinity save God, Muhammad is the Messenger of God'; this testimony to the Muhammadan presence is an affirmation of the religion ensuing from that presence, and for this reason I say: I have naught in me save 'Muhammad is the Messenger of God' (peace and blessings be upon him!). He has said, 'I was a Prophet when Adam was between clay and water.'[36] Every prophet that came before him (peace and blessings be upon him!) had knowledge of those prophets that preceded him as well as knowledge of his own era, so that when our Prophet Muhammad came, (peace and blessings be upon him!) he knew what the prophets before him had known and knew also what would come to pass among the Caliphs after him. Nothing more could be revealed after him, for he was the seal of all the prophets; in him was the function of prophecy completed and the light of sanctity begun. Every saint in existence knows what the prophets and saints knew before him as well as having the wisdom of his own time. The seal of sanctity for its part lies at the feet of Muhammad (peace and blessings be upon him!), for it is a single ray of the all-encompassing Muhammadan Light, a light from the Lights of the Messenger of God (peace and blessings be upon him!) in whom the great sanctity is sealed. After his coming the world will never be without a man to guide all men—one who does not have preferences for one group over another and who is like a flame of spirituality for all."

My honored father was once with Sidi Muhammad al-Antaqli. The latter sat before him without uttering a word. My father said to him: "What is this stiffness in you? Why do you not speak?" He answered, "I am not gifted for speaking. Our brethren in the *ṭarīqa* are rich in this respect, and I am poor in comparison." My father then said, "God has given us intelligence and ordained a straight path for us, which we follow. The law cannot govern him who has no intelligence. You must speak to your soul of good deeds and acts of worship, and let it take pleasure in pleasant things, while warning it and restraining it from what is forbidden." Muhammad al-Antaqli said, "I fear that if I deal gently with it, it will overpower me." "No, no" my father said, "Look at my little daughter Maryam. Every morning when she gets up she points her hand in the direction of the mosque and says, 'God is most great! God is most great!' We have a natural propensity for religion since birth. What has Ibn Ata Allah said in his *Ḥikam*? 'Do not be companion to one whose state does not cause yours to raise, or whose words do not guide you towards God.' Whose state will raise yours and whose words will lead you to God save those of your Shaykh and brethren in God? And if it is difficult for you to be with your Shaykh and to listen to him and to your brethren, then you must sit and learn from the pious doctors of the law."

The saintly Sidi Khalil al-Kurdi related the following to me: "During my retreat in the *zāwiya*, it occurred to me to discipline myself by fasting, so I went forty days without any food, and began to become accustomed to do thus. Then I began to fast three days and in the evening of the last day break my fast on a few dried dates. After some time, however I experienced weakness and fatigue, and went to ask advice from our master. When I mentioned to him that I had fasted, he looked hard at me and said, 'Who told you to do this?' I was silent, and felt filled with shame. He said, 'Do you know, my son, the ego gains access to the soul of the disciple from every gate, even from that of good deeds, making it appear desirable to him to do a certain thing. When the disciple has such an idea, he must present it before his Shaykh; then if he permits him to do it, he may, and if not, he must not. If the Shaykh is absent, he should discuss it with others, saying, my soul is telling me to do such and such. At that, the suggestion will flee and the hold of the ego will be broken. Those who have realized God restrain their egos in this way; for if the disciple speaks of his ego to his brethren, he will surely find among them a rightly guided brother who raises his aspirations to be near God, and someone who extols the prescribed acts of worship, for it is these which strengthen the heart.'"

Among his teachings is that which explains the different levels of the soul. There are seven of them, as follows: the carnal (*al-ammāra*), the blaming (*al-lawwāma*), the inspired (*al-mulhama*), the peaceful (*al-muṭma'inna*), the contented (*al-rāḍiya*), the one which pleases God (*al-marḍiya*), and the perfect (*al-kāmil*). The carnal soul is that which incites its owner to pursue desires, distracts him from religious works, and causes him to give up his abode in the after-life for the sake of the here-below. God has said in His mighty Book: "Verily the human soul incites to evil."[37] The blaming soul belongs to the believer, for he whose heart is dead does not discern between obedience and disobedience. The believer's heart is alive, thus when he obeys his Lord his heart is at ease and happy. When he disobeys Him, it suffers and reproaches the soul so that it will revert to good works. Still, there is, nonetheless, an element of the passionate soul at this level, and for this reason God has said, "And I swear by the blaming soul."[38] The inspired soul is the one of which it says God "inspired it with a consciousness of what is wrong for it and what is right for it";[39] the soul is far from the stations of certainty and steadfastness to the Truth, and he inspired it to knowledge of itself and to strive against its passions, thereby becoming pure. The soul at peace, for its part, has reached the first step towards perfection—it is necessary then for it to be contented, and to be pleasing to God through all that God has decreed for it. Then its owner will be praised for his ascent after having himself been the one who praised God. God most high has said, "O thou soul at peace! Return to thy Lord content, in His good pleasure. Enter thou among My slaves; enter thou My garden."[40] The perfect soul has reached the highest station of worship and its owner is of those who have borne witness to and realized the One. Such are they who serve the most glorious Divinity, outwardly and inwardly, after closing every door to the Devil and refusing to yield to him any power—"And for him who fears the standing before his Lord there are two gardens."[41]

My father (may God be pleased with him!) was extremely kind towards the disciple of humble means, encompassing him with mercy and placing great value on whatever that disciple offered him in the way of God, taking the little they gave to use for himself, and leaving what the other disciples offered him to be spent on the *zāwiya* and to help others of the *ṭarīqa*. It once happened that our brethren in Safad collected some money to give to the *zāwiya*. A group had prepared to bring the money and were on the point of departure when a woman called Um Hamid, who was a disciple of our Shaykh, came to implore them to wait a little while for her to go home and return, for she had been able to save a little money to send with them. But they set off instead without waiting for her and when, upon her return she did not find them, she walked until she finally caught up with them in the village of Ayn Zaytun near Safad, and gave them a quarter of a medjidie.[42] Now the man who was carrying the money feared lest he be ambushed and robbed on the way and so he did not open the cloth bundle to put the coins in it, but rather dropped them into his pocket and thought no more about it. When they reached Acre they went to my honored father, who was seated before a large assembly in the *zāwiya*. They offered him the sum of money and, as was customary, he did not take it himself but told them to hand it to Sidi Mustafa al-Sadi, keeper of the *zāwiya* for him to spend it on the *zāwiya* and the disciples.

Now the one who had brought the money had forgotten about the incident with the woman and that he still had her money in his pocket and he proceeded to take his place among the disciples. Suddenly he heard our Shaykh's voice calling to him and asking, "Where are the coins the poor woman sent to me? I have need of them." The man nearly fell down from astonishment, and rushed forward to offer the trust to my father, kissing his hands and asking him to pardon him and excuse him. Our Shaykh took the money and put it in his pocket. The day the party returned to Safad, the man hastened to see the woman to tell her the good news and related how my father had disregarded the large amount of money and concerned himself only with hers. At this she wept from joy and gratitude.

Our brother, Shaykh Abd al-Raziq related to me: "Our Shaykh did not like to see birds caged, and whenever any birds were brought to the *zāwiya* he ordered either that they be killed straightaway to be eaten or set free to fly in the open air. Now one day one of the disciples gave two quails to Maryam, daughter of the Shaykh. She was just a small child then and was delighted with them. The following day she could no longer find the birds, and became so sad she wept, so I said to her, 'They have gone home to their families, but tomorrow or the day after they will return to us.' Two days later I bought two quails and took them to her right away, saying, 'Here they are, they have come back.' She was overjoyed at this, and while I was speaking with her, the Shaykh came to me and said, 'What is this? Have you brought some quails for Maryam?' 'Yes my lord,' I replied. He said, 'The hunters in my land, the Maghrib, are more adept than those in this country. Their method of capturing quail is to take a live bird in a cage atop a high hill, and lay traps around it, putting grains in each trap. The other birds hear the voice of the bird in the cage, and come to eat the grain, and there they are caught in the trap. It is even thus your Shaykh deals with you: he sets a trap, and places the seed of love of God in it. The bird of the heart comes, and upon perceiving it, throws itself on it. In this way you have all fallen into the net of your Shaykh.'" At this Shaykh Abd al-Raziq said, "May God not set us free from this net!" The following day, our Shaykh ordered that the two new birds be either slaughtered or given their freedom.

My honored mother related to me: "Our Shaykh went to visit the Aqsa mosque in Jerusalem at the invitation of his disciples, and his wife Um Muhy al-Din and her son, who was seven years old, accompanied him. There a notable of the city who was in the *ṭarīqa* invited him to his home. Now this man had a black slave woman who had a small, sickly child not yet three years old, called Jawhar. The gentleman confided in our Shaykh, saying, 'This black, sickly child is my son, and his mother is a slave woman I lawfully possess. However, being such a prominent figure, I cannot admit this for fear of how the child will be treated at the hands of my children and my wife. Thus, I offer him to you to be a companion to Muhy al-Din. When my father returned home he brought the child with him, and he was raised in the spaciousness of the *zāwiya* under the protection of my father and enjoyed his generosity and affection. He was both friend and brother to my brother Muhy al-Din.'" Upon reaching the age of manhood, our Shaykh bought him out of his required military service, married him off, and gave him some land, an orchard of olive trees, and a small house. He supplied him with all he needed to live independently in his house with his family. Jawhar lived extinguished in his love for his Shaykh and in the service of the path and its followers. He was among the greatest of disciples, one who had direct knowledge of God and His Messenger. I saw him in the last days of his life; he came to visit us one day, and I asked him about his lineage and whether he realized that he was descended from nobility. He answered, saying, "The pride I have of being counted among the slaves and servants of your father is sufficient for me; for he is my father, my mother, my family, indeed my entire clan."

Shaykh Asad related another story to me, as follows: "Once, just after my return from Egypt I fell ill with a high fever. I took a book from the library to read called *The Universal Man* (*Al-Insān al-Kāmil*) by Abd al-Karim al-Jili. When I opened it, my eyes fell upon the phrase, 'I am He and He is I,' and I began to repeat this, as I was not strong enough to go on reading more. I put the book back in its place and returned to bed, all the while repeating the phrase, 'I am He and He is I.' No sooner did I lay down in bed again than I lost consciousness. My mother cried out at seeing me thus, and everyone in the house and surrounding street came to see what was wrong. When I came to, I opened my eyes and looked about me in the room. I saw our master, your father standing near my head, smiling. He said, 'If you had been He and He you, you would not have been afflicted by illness.'"

Our life at home in the time of my honored father was one of happiness, carefreeness, and well-being—a life of simplicity, ease, and few complications. Illuminated by the light of faith and good works, it was a life of learning and mystical striving, worship and nobility of character. He (may God be pleased with him!) was a most holy irradiation of the divine Essence, endowed with the nature of the

Messenger of God, walking in his footsteps through all the stations of outward and inward perfections, not lingering at any of them, but understanding the truths in all of them, for he was the Muhammadan heir in all its perfection, immersed in the overflowing bounty of the divine ocean, a perfected, divinely inspired guide. He was an example of devotion towards his parents and family, a generous and noble husband, a gentle and kind father, and a man whose humanity encompassed both men and animals with gentleness and mercy. During the course of his life he married four times, but he never had more than one wife at a time. He had a great respect for women and recognized their rights and duties; moreover, he made efforts to raise their level of knowledge and learning. When he married my honored mother, after his former wife had passed away, she was illiterate so he appointed a private tutor for her to teach her to read and write. After her lessons he used to teach her something of Islamic law, *ḥadīth*, Sufism, and the like, encouraging her to work and serve God, striving in His path to perfection. Thus she attained, by her human and spiritual striving, the highest station in relation to the divine. My father's concern with raising the level of women's spiritual knowledge was not confined to his wives, daughters, and granddaughters; in our house religious lessons were held daily which were attended only by women. My father used to choose a book and a subject, and ask Sayyida Um Ismail al-Dimashqi to give the lesson. Often he would attend the session himself and offer explanations. It was obligatory for all members of our house, as well as those in isolation, visitors, and those living nearby to attend the religious lessons, and it was also obligatory for all the women of our house, even children, to pray five times daily. Every child who was seven years old or more had to pray, fast, and recite the litany. We had a special room for chanting verses of the Quran, where we went every morning, each with her own copy. One of us would read a tenth of the Book aloud, then each one would read whatever amount they could accomplish easily by themselves in a voice so low it was almost a whisper, and after this we would all leave to carry out our household duties. A number of women from aristocratic families of neighboring towns used to visit us, and among the first to receive the initiation from my father was one of these. The circles of invocation which took place in the *zāwiya* were for men only, for my father said, "Circles of invocation are for men, not women." However, this did not mean that women in the *ṭarīqa* were cut off from the practice of the invocation. Every year in Ramadan we prayed the extra prayers in our house, with my father assigning for us a leader in prayer. And after the night prayer or the voluntary prayers we women would recite the Shadhili litany together and then listen to a part of the Quran recited. Thus, I can say that the house in which we lived during the life of my father and afterwards was not only a place of residence, like other homes, but was also like a mosque in which the five prayers were said and the Quran was read in the intervals. My father lived just as the other disciples in his home—praying, reciting the litanies, and giving himself up to worship and obedience, and in addition he was a guide to lead men towards God. He only ceased reciting the litanies with others after he had passed his hundredth year. My sister Maryam once asked him, "My honored father, do you still recite the litanies at your great age, and in your spiritual station?" He replied, "The Messenger of God used to keep vigil at night until his feet were swollen, even after God had forgiven him his former sins and those that were to come. When he was asked concerning this, he said,

'Am I not, then, a grateful servant?'" In the same way, he (may God have mercy on him!) never ceased to get up at night for prayer and vigil up until the night before he passed on to the eternal abode. He spent his time in worship of God night and day, eating and sleeping but little, and living for God and in God. He used to partake of sweetened coffee and tea, and usually went and stayed in the *takīya*, only returning to the house to eat and sleep. At times he ate with his disciples, for he spent most of his time with them, and he prayed the dawn prayer with them in the mosque behind the imam. When he passed his hundredth year, he began to pray it in his room, and then go down to the *takīya* as was his custom. He used to enjoy walking in the fresh air and would pay visits to the tomb of the prophet Salih (peace and blessings be upon him!) or to the tomb of a saintly man of the area.

We used to sleep with him in one room; he was very kind to us, and treated us with the gentlest of fatherly care and the greatest of tenderness. He was concerned with the circumstances of all the women who were in isolation in the house along with the servants and tried to make them happy if possible. It is certain that the women among the disciples who attained realization and knowledge of God and His Messenger—those to whom God gave victory and aid from His Messenger—were so many that there is not space here to write all of their names; suffice it to say that my honored father declared that in the city of Safad alone there were forty women who had realized God.

He used to hold lessons to teach me the holy Quran, and would explain the verses to me in a way that I could easily understand. He would tell me about the reason a verse was revealed, the mark it had left in history on the making of laws, and what it has ordained for the believer regarding works and worship and Sufism; all this was taught in a simple and helpful way and thus he set the foundation for me to begin learning about Islamic culture and Sufism, and it was also the basis for my journey on the path of God, mighty and most high.

On account of his kindness, fairness, and charity to all, he arranged that the little girls who lived in the *zāwiya* take lessons in the Quran as well, so that they might benefit in the same way I did, in spite of the fact that they went to school and I did not. So they sat with me to hear his lectures, and all were treated equally by him. He never forbade me to play with the other little girls of my age when he saw me doing so, but told me to treat those who were disciples like my sisters. Whenever they accompanied me on my daily outings in the carriage, he was kind to them and would offer them something sweet to eat and perhaps a little money. He was always very attentive to me, for he realized that he was an old man while I was still a very young child and that he could pass away before I reached the age of maturity and understanding. He wanted, therefore, to direct me towards the acquisition of knowledge, and towards Sufism and worship, endeavoring to engrave upon my mind images of the Sufi path that would endure in me forever. And so I used to spend much of my time in the company of learned literary men and philosophers. He appointed a pious teacher from those in retreat in the *zāwiya* to take care of me and educate me.

I remember an interesting story about him which I will relate here: He used to be a student of religious studies in Beirut, and had a great aversion for Sufis and Sufism. Thus when his father and brothers entered the Shadhili *ṭarīqa* he was deeply grieved and told them how he felt. Then he went to the Hijaz to make the pilgrimage and to settle there far from his father and brothers. He resided in Medina near the tomb of the Prophet for two years, making the pilgrimage twice, and at the end of his second year he had a vision of the Prophet while sleeping where he told him, "O Salim, if you wish to please me, go to Acre, to Shaykh Ali Nur al-Din al-Yashruti al-Hasani." At this he left immediately and went to see our Shaykh. He received the initiation, and went into retreat in our *zāwiya*. There he married, had children, and remained the rest of his days. My father loved him, for he saw in him righteousness, devotion, and faith; this disciple spent all his time serving and trusting in his Shaykh, extinguished in his love for him. He knew the Quran by heart and had mastered the science of recitation. He was a realized soul, who had attained to the station of nearness to God, and after my father died he lived in our house until his own death. When I was entrusted to his care I was in the spring of my second year. He used to carry me in his arms or in the little children's cart, and take me to attend meetings of spiritual learning, remembrance of God, and to sessions of study as well, so I would not miss anything. Thus I grew up amidst the best of scholars. When my mind first began to open to the light of knowledge, at the age of five, I came to love these meetings of the learned men—I even preferred them to playing with the other children, for they would often relate pleasant and wonderful stories. At this time my father wished for me to attend the religious study circles, both general and specialized, to listen and learn from them what I could. And so I used to sit cross-legged on the floor next to my father, delighted to be near him. It would have been difficult for me to grasp any of these advanced teachings were it not for the fact that my father explained much of the easy things to me at home, and so I began after a long time to gradually understand the explanations, the technical terms, and the allusions and hence a bond of friendship and affection developed between myself and some of these scholars.

He (may God be pleased with him!) raised me as a Sufi and educated me in the way of the *ṭarīqa*. Beginning in my fifth year I prayed at the five prescribed times, and recited the litany with him. He used to wake me up to pray with him in the last part of the night, and when my grandmother would ask him, "What could this child understand from getting up during these cold nights?" he would answer, "I want to impress this image on her mind forever." My father used to get very angry if I made an error in matters of religion or my dealings with others. Only after I had repented of my deed and started afresh would I win his favor again. Although I was just a child, I firmly believed that my father was not as other fathers but was one of God's chosen saints, and whenever I spoke of him it was with veneration and deference. It happened once that I went with Hajj Salim[43] to the seaside. He was fasting that day, and so when the sun was close to setting he said to me, "Come, let us return," but I refused and started to cry, so he gave in reluctantly and we remained there until after the time of the night prayer. When we finally returned home we found the gate locked from the inside, contrary to the usual habit. We called to the doorkeeper to let us in, but he told us, "Our master had ordered me not to let you in." I was very young at the time and became extremely upset, saying to Hajj Salim, "Where can I go?" Then just at that moment, my older sister Aisha came to the gate and let me in. After I had kissed my father's hands and expressed my sorrow and contrition, he said, "Did you not know that Hajj Salim was fasting and that he must not remain until this late hour without food? Such is disobedience of the holy law. What is more, he could be suffering and hungry. If you do not feel the sufferings of others as your own suffering, then I do not want to have you as my daughter."

In another instance, my mother had a relative—a child who was an orphan and was the same age as I. She wanted the child to be my companion, but I refused to have her, saying, "This child is quick to anger, and I will not be able to bear her quarreling." My mother became angry and at that moment my father entered the room and seeing her thus, asked me what had happened. I related the conversation to him and when I was finished he said, "I would not have thought that you would refuse such an act of humanity—you, who are my daughter. I do not want you to leave this girl feeling the marks of her bereavement throughout her life because of the loss of her father." And so I became content with this and she and I lived together until she was married.

He (may God be pleased with him!) directed me towards good works and righteous acts since my earliest youth. It once happened that there was a poor family living near the *zāwiya*. The father was a gambler, a drunkard, and a boisterous, wasteful fellow. His daughter used to come and play with me, and one day I saw her crying. She told me that her family had not eaten for two days, and that her father did not care for them. I told her to follow me to my house and bring a pot. She came along with her elder brother and when we got to the house we filled up the pot with food for them and gave her enough bread for the whole family. My father saw me at this and calling me to him, asked what I was doing. When I told him he encouraged me, and said a prayer asking God to bestow goodness and blessings upon me. Then he said, "That is not enough. You must undertake the support of this family, and provide your friend with the clothing and food she will need for a full year." So I used to take money and give it to them myself, and things remained in this way until my father passed on to meet his Lord. Thus he raised me to be generous and to respect people. Whenever I asked him for something he granted it to me, provided I did not exceed the bounds of courtesy or of the religious law. If I asked a favor of him for myself or on the part of one of our brethren, it was granted and my mediation proved to be helpful for some. He would get angry if the disciples called their children or grandchildren by the title "Sidi," for he said this was not to be used for children who were not disciples themselves; they should be called simply by their names. At the same time, he knew very well that he was going to leave myself and my sister, two small children, with "no might or power" save in God. For this reason, he introduced me to the most senior disciples, to scholars, doctors of the law and to our saintly brethren so that we would share affection and fellowship in God and they would feel kindness and respect for us which would grow and blossom with the passage of time, for affection does not necessitate physical proximity, but physical proximity is always in great need of true affection. Thus he did not object if a disciple called me by the title "Sayyida" but was content to smile at it. At times he showed his affection for me by saying: "I fill Fatima's heart," meaning that my love for him filled my heart. In my eyes, this was a glory above all others; to see that he perceived in my heart the sincerity of my love—that love which is for me the central point of the path.

Our brother Sidi So-and-so once related to me: "When you were a little girl I was very fond of you, and our Shaykh never permitted anyone but Hajj Salim to carry you or take care of you, as he was the one honored with the task of educating you in all fields of learning. He and I were companions, and he trusted me and at times allowed me to carry you, which was never forbidden by your honored father. Now one day your father said to me, 'Beware lest you disobey Fatima.' I replied, 'I hear and will obey.' Several days later while I was walking through the *zāwiya* with you on my shoulders your father called me. I was on the point of answering his call when you said, 'Stay where you are. Do not go to him.' So I remained standing in my spot, not moving. The Shaykh looked and approaching me, said, 'I called you, did you not hear me?' 'O yes,' I replied, 'but I obeyed Sayyida Fatima's orders; did you not tell me to do so?' He was pleased with my answer, and prayed that I be given blessings and goodness."

Some of his Counsels

He said: "He who is present (with God) has knowledge of that which is outside (of Him). The most important basis of our noble *ṭarīqa* and its foundation is the realization of God, blessed and most high, through His Names, His attributes, His actions and prescriptions, and through His aspects and levels of manifestation. One must manifest these elements in their entirety by discerning between the levels of reality in each of His modes of perfection which belong in turn to each of His degrees. To go no further than the station of unity—that which is the station of extinction—and to call this station the highest divine station—is ignorance and error and removes one from the more exalted realm of the Real; the sincere disciple must go out from the night of ignorance and find the light of discernment; he must attribute to the divine stations their true levels of reality so that the treasury of secrets be opened to him beyond the pavilions of veils and illusions, and so that his realization bears witness to the Truth, the essence of all the other manifestations. To reach this, however, the disciple must devote himself to what his master orders and avoid what he forbids him. If not, these stations and wisdom will vanish, and the wisdom of the noble Messengers (peace and blessings be upon them!) will have been taught to no avail. The pillars of the religion will be destroyed, the gift of the masters will be lost, and forgetfulness will steal into the hearts of the rebellious, disobedient ones.... The sincere seeker is obliged to love his Shaykh, for he believes him to be the Muhammadan heir and to be his representative because of the wisdom granted to him through his isolation from the world and his obedience to His commands, and because he is submitted to Him, outwardly and inwardly."

Before his journey to his Lord, he said, "We came from our land in order to teach you about God, and we have accomplished this; God the glorious is the Ever-Present and Eternal; so cleave to Him and take refuge with Him. Do not be negligent in your invocation of the Name. Be as one heart and one soul. Do not change in your attitudes towards one another, or become separated; remain as you are, and take as an example what we have taught you and avoid what we have prohibited to you. Do not say that we have left you; we are present, and are watching you. Do not say, we do not see you, for by God, we for our part see you and know the state of each one of you.

"Every prescription of the exoteric law contains within it a treasure from the divine reality, which can only be obtained by first having a perfect understanding of these prescriptions.

"The water of the ocean was sweet in its primordial form; but when an element of the relative and accidental came into it, it became salty. One must be an intelligent master to purify it and restore it to its original state.

"Observe those who recite the Quran. Every man reads his particular chapter, for all of existence is a proof of God (*furqān*); he whose reading (Quran) has been surpassed by his proofs of God (*furqān*), has perfected his faith and understanding.

"All of existence is the Book; the prophets are its chapters; the greatest of the Muslims and the infidels are its verses; the greater part of creation are its words; the lower levels of existence are its letters, and the totality is Allāh.

"A state in man is of almost imperceptible duration, and his life is the sum of his individual states. At each instant he is created anew; no sooner is one state given life than another follows in a new creation; thus it is that man has been created from naught. He is but a ray of life issuing from the divine Void, and he is real to the extent that he possesses wisdom which unites him to God.

"The servant does not cease to invoke God until the Supreme Name (*Allāh*) takes possession of him. When this happens, servanthood is absorbed into Lordship and the qualities of the Lord manifest themselves in him, and in rapture for the Divinity he forgets his outward and inward existence.

"When unitive knowledge (*al-jam*ᶜ) takes possession of the inner depths of the disciple, the springs of divine wisdom gush forth from his heart to his tongue, and because of this, there are those who have been tortured or killed for speaking of this station. The soul of him who has only separative knowledge (*farq*) on the other hand will run past his spiritual possibilities like water through a green reed.

"The path is like a jewel hidden in a box. The key to it is the remembrance of God, and the mold of the key is the restraint of the senses from wrongdoing.

"The invocation cleanses the heart of all impurities; remember God with consciousness of the One; He will remember thee by supporting thee. Remember God in gratitude, He will remember thee with abundance. Remember Him with obedience, He will remember thee with grace. Remember Him with love, He will approach near to thee.

"Verily God illumines His beloved just as the sun illumines the earth—above, in the clear sky, it sheds its light upon the earth. Would the earth therefore ever be permitted to say, 'I am the sun'?! Certainly not! This could never happen—what a great difference exists between them!

"Love God by obedience to His Messenger (peace and blessings be upon him!) and let your love of the latter ripen in your hearts; for whoever is in need of spiritual nourishment will benefit by this. Love God with a love that makes you oblivious of your corporeal and sensible existence, and thus become of those who abide only in His angelic domain. Love came before all else, for it was the first thing that issued forth from the divine Essence. It has no end and is eternal, abiding on earth through its Muhammadan manifestation."

In explanation of the *ḥadīth*, "The things that have been made lovable to me in this world are women and perfume. And I have been given refreshment through prayer," he said: "Women represent the divine infinitude, perfume is what emanates from them, and prayer is a vision of their essences." In another version he said, "Women are the manifestations of possibilities, perfume the good that is in them, and prayer is perfect consciousness of their essences."

The Expansion of the *Ṭarīqa*

Many are astonished and wonder at the speed with which our *ṭarīqa* spread through so many countries after my honored father went from the west to the east. Within two years after his arrival the *ṭarīqa* had spread all throughout greater Syria—meaning Syria, Lebanon, Palestine, and Trans-Jordan. In fact, though, this is not so strange when one considers the wisdom and principles of the *ṭarīqa* and the nature of its Shaykh, dignitaries, and saintly disciples. All of these contributed to its rapid spread, and all who chose to attach themselves to our Shaykh and follow his path were destined to do so even before they left the world of the spirit and entered the world of forms. Some of them were to attain the ultimate goal, not stopping at the knowledge of the attributes, but persevering to reach the divine Essence. In some this light was manifest while in others it was hidden from the outward by veils. The Sufi masters (may God be pleased with them!) believe that one can measure the power of the signs of guidance and the level of sanctity of the sage not by looking at the masses and simple people who followed him, for these are quick to accept anything; it is rather measured by how much it attracts to the path the hearts of the great theologians living in the age of the saint. Thus, one has said, "To be a true Shaykh is not to guide fifty ordinary men, but one learned man," and it is well known that the strength of the doctors of the law should not be underestimated, for when they can encompass both the outward and inward realms of knowledge in themselves they can help many through their wisdom and are one of the pillars of Sufism. Of the graces bestowed upon my honored father (may God be pleased with him!) was that his saintliness was known far and wide by all classes and races of men. God honored him with powerful signs from Him, and he attracted many of the greatest scholars of his time. They had a great influence on others while in the service of the *ṭarīqa* and its members. God guided their actions and their qualities became one with His. He revealed unto them His secrets, and gave them realization of Him.

Sayyida Fatima's Life

I was born in 1891 and raised in my father's *zāwiya*—that of the Shadhili Yashruti in Acre, Palestine. When I was born, my father was one hundred years old, and this occasion caused much celebration in our house and in the *zāwiya*, for my honored father did not have many surviving children. He passed on to the next world when I was just eight years old. There was a woman in our *zāwiya* who was thought by all to be a very pious person, so when my mother gave birth to me, my father went to her and said, "I would like you to give me a blessed name for my child which I have at last been given," and she replied, "Is there any more noble name than that of your grandmother Sayyidatna Fatima al-Zahra (may God be pleased with her!), daughter of the Prophet?" And thus I was honored with that noble name.

It was always a source of pride and happiness to me that I bore a great physical resemblance to my father; I was given the same shape of face and cheekbones, similar facial features and nose, and a white complexion. My hands, with their long fingers and fair complexion are also inherited from him. Whoever saw me as a child knew that I was the Shaykh's daughter on account of our great likeness.

The *zāwiya* in Acre was a meeting place for men of learning and law, of Sufism and gnosis. Ever since my eyes first saw the light of day I found myself living among these learned men and attending study circles, spiritual counsels, and meetings of scholars and lawyers. My father favored me and by his kindness to me directed me towards those fields of religious education which emphasized learning and Sufism and which encompassed outward and inward knowledge. Thus he had me sit in those circles of Sufi learning where he spoke and which the most learned theologians attended. I began to do this regularly when I was four years old and was the only child and the only female who devoted herself to lessons of this sort. My father was well aware that he would leave myself and my sister all alone in the world and so he wanted to have me start my pursuit of knowledge of religion and Sufism, to which my life was to be devoted in the future. This explains the extraordinary attention with which he guided me towards these domains.

My sister Maryam was born two years after me, that is, at the beginning of 1893. We lived under the care of my father and mother when we were children, then under the care of my mother after my father departed to Paradise, and then together after my mother died, until Maryam left this world to meet her Lord in 1975. I remember a story about her which is as follows: When she was a small child, no more than one year old, she used to hear the voice of the man making the call to prayer, "God is most great! God is most great!" Upon this she would raise her hands over her head and say "*Allāh*!" meaning "God is most great!" Thus was my sister in all the aspects of her life. When she reached the age of six she began to show signs of one traveling on the path, for my mother told me that after getting into bed and going to sleep, my sister used to wake up every night, sit up in her bed, look around her, and ask, "What is the explanation of such and such a verse from such and such a chapter?" The women in the room would awaken, struck with awe, and say nothing. Then my sister would begin explaining the verse and her explanation would be correct, according to those listening. Then she would ask those present, "What is the meaning of such and such a *ḥadīth*?" Again, the women would remain silent in amazement. My sister would then give the explanation of the *ḥadīth*, what happened in it, and its chain of transmission. She would remain thus for some time until sleep once more overcame her. The next morning those who had heard her would ask about what had happened the preceding night, but she knew nothing of what she had done and it was as though she had experienced nothing unusual. She continued in this way for four months, and eventually my mother became very upset and often wept for her. Finally she decided to ask my sister what she saw when she was in that state. One night after my sister had gone to bed, and then awoke, sat up and begun explaining verses of the Quran, they asked her what she saw, and she said, "She sees before her wide, green fields in which there are many people listening to her, and at her side is a man carrying a wreath radiant with light which he wishes to place on her head." My mother said to her, "Tell them 'My mother is sad, she does not want this for me, but wants me to be as I am in the daytime and she pleads with you and asks God for help so that you help her.'" My sister began to repeat this. The wish was repeated for ten nights until God accepted my mother's desire and my sister ceased to have these experiences. God the glorious had brought her back from the station of states (*aḥwāl*) to that of perfect sobriety (*ṣaḥw*). My sister combined both the beautiful and the majestic in her character, and was the embodiment of mercy. She ascended the ladder of the path with humility through the stations, witnessing and unveiling the Truth, for she resembled her father both outwardly and inwardly.

My father used to sit and devote himself to the prolonged invocation of the name of God (*Allāh*) while facing the *qibla*.[44] At these times I often sat next to him, for I wished to see him in this state.

The special circumstances in my life seldom permitted me to play with other children my age. This did not upset me, however, for I felt happy and proud to sit with the learned men before my honored father, attending his lessons. Of course I was not completely prevented from having close friends who were dear to me during my childhood. My father, too, was kind to them; he treated them with gentleness and told me to behave with kindness towards them.

Once, when I was six years old, I asked my mother, "Who created me?" "God," she answered. "And who created you?" I asked. "God," she said. "And who created my father?" "God." "And who created our Prophet Muhammad?" "God," she said. "And who created God?" "No one created Him," she said, "He has always existed, even before creating us." "How was He before He created us?" I asked, and she said, "Ask your father." At that moment he was sitting in the same room as us, and was reciting the litany, rosary in hand. I stood before him, kissed his hand, and repeated to him what I had said to my mother. Whenever I asked him about anything, he gave me a complete answer, as though one of his senior disciples were asking, and now when I asked him my question as I had done to my mother, he looked at me, smiling, and repeated the *ḥadīth* of the Prophet (peace and blessings be upon him!) as follows: "He was in darkness. Beneath Him was air and above Him air, and He created His Throne upon the water."[45] Then he closed his eyes, completely absorbed, and continued narrating the *ḥadīth*, his hands resting on his knees.

I was very intimately linked with my father. I accompanied him physically and spiritually wherever he was, whether at home, in the *takīya*, in the prayer room, or out in towns or villages. I remember now how he used to go to the Friday prayer and to the two feast day prayers accompanied by huge groups of disciples. I remember how I used to go with him, never parting from him, saying the prayer behind the *imām* along with the others. At times I went up with Hajj Salim to the roof of the mosque to pray with the men who gave the call to prayer.

One of the dearest memories I have of my childhood is of a dream I had one night while asleep in my bed. I saw the Prophet (peace and blessings be upon him!) lying very still, asleep in my father's bed. Upon seeing him I was seized with a great fear and began to cry and shout out: "O my father! O my lord, O my master, O my grandfather, O my beloved, O Messenger of God!" At this he opened his eyes, and looked at me, smiling. Then he sat up in the bed, drew me to himself and held me to his noble chest, blessing me, and I could feel his breaths entering with mine into my breast. The next morning when I told my father of the vision I had, his eyes filled with tears and he wept from joy, saying to me, "God will give you victory, my daughter, by the grace of those pure, noble breaths." On another night I once again had a vision while asleep, and when I awoke in the morning, I set off to look for my father to tell him of it. I found him that day standing with a group of visiting disciples outside the door to the great hall of the *zāwiya*. I approached him and said, "O my lord! I saw in my sleep that I was standing before the gate of Paradise. The guardian angel opened the gate, and called to me, saying, 'Enter.' 'I will not enter,' I said. 'Why?' he asked. 'I will not enter until Hajj Salim Baliq enters.' 'Then let him enter,' the summoner said. Still I remained where I was and did not enter. I heard the summoner say a second time, 'Enter.' I replied, 'I will not enter.' 'Why?' he asked. 'I will only enter when all of our brethren have entered,' I said, and he replied, 'Then let them enter.' It was then I awoke." When my father heard this, his eyes were filled with tears, and I heard him say to our brethren, "My daughter Fatima is a true disciple, for she loves all brethren in the Path—may my Lord grant her victory!"

On the sixteenth night of Ramadan, in the year 1316 of the Hijra,[46] my father said his obligatory rites, then stayed awake and kept vigil for half of the night in spite of being one hundred and eight years old at the time. He then retired to his bed which was in the same room in which he worshiped, and there, in perfect repose and silence, he left this world to meet his Lord just before the dawn. He was one who had pleased God and whose soul was in peace, for he had possessed confidence in God to the greatest possible degree and had spent his entire life in the service of the primordial (*ḥanīf*) religion by guiding aspirants and spreading the *ṭarīqa* far and wide. As I mentioned earlier, my relationship with my father was founded upon veneration, respect, and great spiritual love, and because of this love which filled all my thoughts and my heart, I am helpless to describe here the extent of the grief and pain I felt upon his passage to the everlasting Paradise. From the moment the news of his death reached my ears, I felt as though I had fallen from heaven down to earth, and I left our house and went to the *zāwiya*, wandering without knowing where I was going. It is true of course that I was only eight years old when my father passed away, but whoever had lived as I had, in his shadow and among the most eminent leaders in thought and learning, and whoever had enjoyed guidance such as his would no doubt have experienced the events and changes which came to pass not as a small child, but as an adult possessed of a fully mature mind.

I can remember that on the third day after my father passed away, I was afflicted with an illness which confined me to my bed as a result of my extreme grief and pain. While in bed I picked up the Quran and began reading the chapter of *The Cave*. I came to the verse which says, "...and their father had been righteous, and thy Lord intended that they should come to their full strength and should bring forth their treasure as a mercy from their Lord...."[47] Upon reading this verse I felt a great peace entering my soul, bringing rest to my mind and calm to my wounded heart, and I realized at that moment that God, glorious and most high, would not forsake me, and that my father's care for me ever since I came into this world was a clear proof that God had taken my hand and would guide my footsteps and illuminate my heart so that I would be shown what was best for me in my religious and worldly life.

I was afraid that after my father's death I would lose the opportunity to attend meetings of scholars and doctors of the law and that I could no longer go to the study circles which were attended by scholars and Sufis who came from various parts of the city and from distant towns to hear my father's discourses, explanations, and interpretations. However, fortunately my link with these learned men was not broken at all after his death; in fact, they became even kinder to me and my sister. The bonds between us were strengthened and the roots of our relationship deepened and remained strong throughout my life. Such friendship had a great impact upon me and was to have an influence on the formation of my character. As our master Shaykh Taj al-Din ibn Ata Allah al-Iskandari said (may God be pleased with him!) in his *Ḥikam*: "Do not befriend one whose state does not inspire you, or whose words do not lead you to God." This was the direction towards which my father had led me and which he wished me to follow.

Without doubt, it was my mother who helped the most to nurture the growth of the Sufi spirit in myself and my sister after my father's departure from this earthly life. She always urged us to practice what he had desired of us, and one of the things which helped us realize our goal was the existence of a library at the *zāwiya* containing precious and valuable books, as well as a private library of my father's in our house. Although still very young, I decided to try to read many of these books so that through their instruction I might obtain of my father's teaching what I would otherwise have missed.

I remember that I asked my mother for permission to veil myself in front of the great scholars and in front of our brethren disciples of my father. She consulted with my brother Ibrahim and with those scholars and brethren we knew and they all agreed that I should not be permitted to use the veil while with them. She did permit me, however, to dress as I had done in the days of my father, when I used to meet these men in our house wearing a wide, white prayer scarf on my head. In the street I went veiled like the rest of the young ladies of the day, for in that time this practice was observed most strictly.

I cannot be certain at what point in my life I learned to write. Moreover, I do not remember sitting before a teacher and learning it from him, and cannot recall the first time I ever picked up a pen. All I can remember is that I wanted to learn to write ever since I began to understand the nature of things, and after my father's death I used to see Hajj Salim writing letters to his family. I would take one of these letters, put a thin piece of paper over it, and trace on to it what he had written in his letter. He would watch me doing this, and after some weeks he asked me, "What are you doing, mistress?" "I am drawing the word on the thin paper," I replied, "I am just playing with it." He said, "Are you able to understand the meaning of the words you are writing?" "Yes," I said, "Have you forgotten that I have completed the Quran and know some of its verses by heart?" He said, "Then read what you have written." So I read it, and he said, "Now I will write a line for you and you copy it out for me." So I tried and succeeded in copying it without using the thin paper. Hajj Salim went on teaching me to write in this way, and in time I learned, and that is why my handwriting resembles Hajj Salim's. I remember that after I wrote the first line Hajj Salim went to tell the good news to my mother, saying, "My lady! Little Fatima has learned to write by herself by the blessings of her father." My mother was very happy at this, as was everyone else in the house at that time.

The home in which a child is raised has a great and lasting influence on her and determines to a large degree the formation of her personality. I remember my sister Aisha, the first born of my father, when she was about ninety years old. I never saw her without a book in her hand. In her free time she used to see to her religious duties, reciting the litanies and invoking the name of God (*Allāh*). Then after this she spent most of her time reading books. She not only read religious works on theology and Sufism, but also books on history, literature, and ancient and modern poetry. She was very happy to see me at the age of nine or ten with so much determination, working hard to read as much as possible to increase in wisdom and learning. My mother feared that I read too much, especially during my severe bouts of asthma, but my sister Aisha used to say to her, "Let her read, she will attain greatness in society and in the *ṭarīqa*, if God most high wills. This strong motivation to acquire knowledge even when just a young child has to manifest itself somehow in the world. My sister will obtain that which she desires, with God's permission."

In my father's *zāwiya* there were a number of Quranic reciters who knew the holy Book by heart and who were well known for their beautiful voices. I grew up loving to listen to the recitation of verses of the wise Book and to hear the songs and rhymed poems which were composed. In this way I memorized many verses of the Quran as well as Sufi songs and poems, and I began to have a taste for the arts, poetry, and music in an age in which there were no radios, televisions, or tape recorders.

As I entered my adolescence, God granted me recovery from my asthma, from which I had suffered constantly for ten years. However, because of my prolonged illness I never regained a strong constitution and was in need of care and supervision the rest of my life with respect to food, rest, and social activities. The doctors had advised for my benefit that we spend time in coastal and inland areas, and in lowlands and mountains so as to have a periodical change of climate. Thus, we would journey each year in the spring and summer to the mountains of Palestine, Lebanon, and Damascus, and continued this way up until war broke out in Western Tripoli, waged by the Italians who brought their troops into Beirut and were defeated by the Ottoman Turkish army. During this time it was dangerous to remain near the coast and everyone living in such areas was anxious, especially in the city of Acre, which was still a fortified town of military importance. Many of the inhabitants of that city left to live in nearby villages and mountain areas, fearing an attack by the Italians. After passing a few weeks with our family in fear and apprehension, we decided that there was no alternative but to follow the course of other citizens of Acre. We asked leave of my brother Ibrahim, and then went with my mother, Maryam my sister, and my cousins Anisa and Abda to the *zāwiya* in the mountain village of Tarshiha, twenty-four kilometers northeast of Acre. It was cold up in the mountains and the village even had snow during some of its winters. When we went there it was the beginning of March, and we traveled over a rough, unpaved road. We stayed there three months and during this period my health became worse and I suffered a relapse because of the cold weather. Added to this was the fact that I did not like living in this village, especially in my youth, for I had too many dear memories of spending the summer months there with my father, and receiving huge groups of visitors from various parts of Syria who came to seek his counsel. Were it not for the Italian war which forced me to stay there for three months, I would have preferred to go to the mountains of Lebanon.

Wherever we went on our seasonal trips, my father's disciples would welcome us with joy and celebration and show great affection towards us, as a reminder to us that they remained devoted and full of love for my father, adhering to his teachings and directions in spite of his passing away to the next world.

Throughout our lives our mother never forbade us anything that gave us pleasure, provided it was in conformity with the noble path and the accomplishment of God's commands. We were, praise be to God, the objects of trust, esteem, and respect of whoever we met, whether they were disciples of my father or acquaintances from outside the *ṭarīqa*.

Life in Acre was unsettled after the establishment of the "nation of unity and progress" in Turkey.[48] I used to spend a few weeks there and then go to Haifa, alternating between the two, and in the spring we often went to Sidon or Damascus, or took an excursion in Palestine. People in our country had joined forces four months before the declaration of war by the Ottoman government on the Allies in 1914. At that time I was suffering from a gastric fever, and so my mother decided that we should go to stay in Damascus for the duration of the war. They waited for me to recover, and when I had partially overcome my sickness but was still feeling weak, we prepared to leave the city. However, we could not find any carriage or animal to convey us to the train station which lay outside Acre in order to travel by it to Haifa and on to Damascus, for the Ottoman army had already taken possession of all the means of communication and transportation in the region. I was still too weak to go by foot from our house in the old city to the train station, so my cousin Sidi Hasan carried me there in his arms. We were very sad to have to leave the city which housed the remains of my father, although at that time we did not think that we would be kept away for long, and had hope that we would surely be able to return to our beloved city one day. My mother, my sister Maryam, and my cousin Anisah traveled with me, while my brother Ibrahim remained in Acre with his family, along with my cousin Sidi Hasan.

The war gave rise to poverty, hunger, destruction, disease, and the death of multitudes of people. And even though during the First World War our country did not become very involved with the armies engaged in battle, our people suffered deeply from the hardships that resulted from it. The Arab regions of Syria were swept by a wave of typhoid at that time, and I remember during my stay in Damascus there was severe hunger among many that grew worse day by day, especially during the last two years of the war. It became a common sight to see men starve and die in the street, and whenever we went out of the house we saw men, women, and children in distress crying, "We are hungry! We are hungry!"

When I was in Damascus in my youth I would receive the scholars, doctors of the law, and learned men of that city, and during the war, others who had fled from Acre to Damascus. When I met with them I wore the complete veil according to the religious law. My presence in Damascus in that period, and my freedom in the realm of law and the arts afforded me a precious opportunity, for being acquainted with many of the learned men of the time, I was able to broaden my understanding and deepen my knowledge in diverse subjects. I developed a strong and independent personality that has endured in me throughout my life. It was my great good fortune that I was able to take advantage of the opportunity to stay in Damascus at that time, for it was in those days an important center for Islamic scholars in various religious and social domains.

Following the end of World War I, with its grief and misery, people throughout the country once more felt safe and returned to their normal way of life, going back to the homes which they had fled. We for our part returned to our home in Acre, along with many others, and took up our permanent residence there as before the war. From time to time we would take trips to Damascus or Lebanon to visit friends or for a vacation, and then return to our home. In addition we often spent the winter months in Cairo, center of religion, law, literature, and the arts. The first time we went there was in 1920, just after the war. We traveled by train from Palestine and were some of the first women to go to Egypt following the war. During our stay in Cairo we rented a house in the new part of the city, which was at that time no more than a small village. The house that we found for ourselves there became like a miniature *zāwiya*, for we met there with other disciples as well as with scholars and literary men. The situation was similar among my female companions; we occupied ourselves with reading both ancient and contemporary works, works translated from other languages, as well as literary and scholastic journals, and when we met we would discuss our readings. The majority of my companions were gifted women of literary and writing abilities—some were poets and members of the highest ranks of the women's revival movement.

In the years following the war, the eyes of the people were opened to the true nature of what had happened to them. Revolution had come to Egypt in the time of Sa'd Zaghlul, followed by revolution in Damascus, other regions of Syria, and hints of it in Palestine. Thus, we did not feel settled no matter where we were. There was a manifest need for women to be seen more in order for them to participate in the organization and planning of Arab society. In spite of this ambiance I always tended towards a Sufi perspective, which is not surprising, for I saw myself as a *faqīra* of God, majestic and powerful, through my journeying on the straight path and through my love for knowledge, realization, and learning. My father (may God sanctify his secret!) is my master and guide, and I have made great efforts to guard the filial and spiritual link with him. However, I had certain physical weaknesses in those early days which gave rise to the illnesses that afflicted me and to my health condition, and called for special attention. Thus I have lived a fragile life, one in which my schedule of eating, sleeping, and meeting with visitors have all been regulated, and thus I was never able to live in a town cut off from contact with the outside world, or in one where there were no doctors and medicines available, in spite of my attraction to and love for the beauty of nature.

I kept company only with people of learning, mystical knowledge, and the arts; this was not out of any egotism or pride on my part but because I had sat among them and learned from my father since I was a child, and the valuable lessons I heard in those meetings on all aspects of learning had given rise to this tendency in my soul. I was drawn to these worthy scholars and felt a desire deep within my heart to be where they were, and this is what compelled me to return time and again to the cities of Damascus and Cairo, for it was in these important centers that such scholars were to be found.

I was strict with myself, keeping watch over my soul to the extreme limit of conservativeness; I never for one day interrupted saying my prayers or reciting the litanies, even when I was traveling to Cairo, Damascus, or Lebanon, and I set aside times when I went into seclusion to invoke God's name (*Allāh*). In these moments I felt a feeling of peace that I cannot describe adequately in words except to say my soul was engulfed by a most profound feeling of contentment. This was indeed the station of worship (*ᶜubudiyya*) of God the Creator, the One. He has said, "Worship thy Lord until certitude cometh to thee."[49]

In another domain of my life at this time I had women friends, daughters of aristocratic families who had an appreciation for the arts. We used to meet together for singing, socializing, and to discuss various subjects. We would listen to the songs of some who were blessed with beautiful voices, or had skill in rendering a piece of music according to its proper rhythm and melody. Thus I passed the period after World War I.

I did not forget to worship and persevere in Sufi practices, but at the same time I did not cut myself off from the social world which surrounded me and of which I was a part. My relations with many of the great scholars and saintly people were strengthened, and by the grace of God I was confident and secure in all that I did at that time.

It is well known to those familiar with history that the Palestinian revolution raged fiercest in the year 1936, and during that year there was great violence, fighting, and rioting. It was a year that was different from the rest of the years of the revolution and was therefore called the "Revolution of '36." The general history of this affair I leave to historians, and will only include what happened to me and my family during this period, which went on for nearly three years, and which lasted until just before the breakout of World War II in 1939.

When the revolution of '36 broke out I was recovering from a bout of dysentery which had afflicted me two years earlier. At the time I had come down with it, it took a great toll on me, for I already had a weak constitution due to the asthma that I had suffered from in my youth. This illness caused me great discomfort and pain, and my overall health was very slow to recover. At that time I was still living with my mother and sister in Acre, and when the former saw that my health was not improving at all, she decided that we should go to Beirut and seek the advice of well-known doctors there. She was, moreover, urged by the events taking place in Palestine at the time. And so we left for Beirut in the beginning of 1935 and rented a house there. Thus when the worst of the Palestinian revolution came in 1936 I was in Beirut recovering from my illness. It was necessary for me to watch over my health carefully for a few years before I regained my strength, and even then I was delicate and susceptible for a long time. Both my stay in Beirut, that city of learning and intellectuality, and my confinement to my house, encouraged me to read a great deal about various subjects. I benefited from learning more of various ideas and views in different fields. This stay also enabled me to meet with several philosophers and scholars, either through their visits to our house or by attending their lectures, if my health permitted. Thus in this period I was able to increase my store of knowledge, particularly in the domain of philosophy and in the realm of Sufism.

After we had spent nearly three years in Beirut during the period of the revolution, World War II was declared. A few weeks after, we left Beirut and moved to Damascus, but after two months returned to Lebanon, for it had become clear to us that we could not stay there during winter as it was extremely cold, and my mother was no longer young and needed to see the doctors in Beirut with whom she was accustomed and who were familiar with the details of her health condition. Thus we stayed the summer in the city of Aliya in the mountains and the winter months in Beirut on the coast. In spring we traveled either to Acre or Damascus, depending upon the conditions of transportation at the time. Days, months, and years passed thus, traveling from one city to another and hoping to be able to return to our country and live in Acre after the war.

At the end of the third year of the war, I sat down one day to write some letters. In fact, however, without intending to, I wrote a discourse on Sufism of over seven pages in length.

I was amazed at what I had done, and felt that a spirit, or rather a hidden voice had urged me to write about the path and about my father and his Sufic message (may God sanctify his secret!). The moment I finished writing these pages I hastened to show them to my mother, who encouraged me, saying, "Do as you are ordered. This is a fruit of the blessings your father bestowed upon you." I remembered then what my friends who were doctors of the law and scholars had asked of me, namely, to write a book which would relate the story of my father's life, his deeds, and his message. I knew then that the duty of writing this book had fallen to me, and that I would confirm what had come to pass in his life and tell of the grace God had bestowed upon him. Thus I began to write my first book which was entitled *Journey to the Truth.* This work begins with an introduction to Sufi doctrine, followed by a description of my father's doctrine, his life and influence on Sufism, and something about the Shadhili *ṭarīqa.* I remember that, when writing some of the chapters of this book, it was necessary for me to refer to some of the books of the Sufi masters. Now in spite of my complete faith in the sanctity of Shaykh Muhy al-Din ibn Arabi (may God be pleased with him!), I neglected to make use of his valuable works, for I thought: Shaykh Muhy al-Din has some enemies, and I do not want to open the door of dispute by referring to him. From the moment this thought passed through my mind, I was no longer able to continue writing—my hand was paralyzed for three years, unable to complete the work without knowing why. Then one day a woman disciple from Damascus came to visit us in Beirut, and during her stay she saw my father in her sleep one night. She kissed his hand in her vision, and asked him why I had stopped writing. He answered, saying, "Because Fatima has closed the door upon

Shaykh Muhy al-Din, may God be pleased with him!" The next morning, this disciple related her vision to me. I asked forgiveness of God and repented for my erroneous thought. Then I hastened to the books of Shaykh Muhy al-Din and began to read them and absorb their wisdom. During my study of his works I came across a poem which he wrote called Journey to the Truth. This title pleased me and I gave it to my book as well, guided by Shaykh Muhy al-Din's example. The writing of my first book took just under fourteen years to complete. I wrote down what came back to me in all humility and devotion, telling of the graces which our *ṭarīqa* enjoyed. I only wrote when I felt composed in the depths of my soul, and then I would seclude myself in my room to record my memories and to write about what I had learned of Sufism.

After the Second World War ended, we decided to remain living in Beirut, as we had grown accustomed to life there and it had become an absolute necessity to have a doctor nearby, especially for my mother. However, we still used to visit our home in Acre once or twice a year for a few weeks during spring or autumn. We remained thus until the great Palestinian disaster of 1948, when we were compelled along with most other Palestinians to flee from our homes—an emigration from which we have not been able to return to this day.

My new permanent residence in Beirut afforded me the opportunity to continue pursuing intellectual activities in spite of my delicate health, for this city was and still is one of the most important centers of learning and thought in the Arab world. The existence of several universities, along with the freedom of thought, speech, and publishing which existed there, encouraged diverse views and beliefs to manifest and interact with each other either through the medium of newspapers, magazines, books, or in lectures and debates. Life in Beirut differed from that of other Arab countries, for groups of people from different nations and regions had immigrated there, and each of these groups had its own customs, traditions, and way of thinking, so that if one observes the events of life in Beirut he will not be able to decide whether he is in an oriental or a western country, so distinct and peculiar is its character. The absolute and unbounded freedom of thought, speech, and deeds can reach a point of near chaos. There were those of this beautiful city who advocated the adoption of western urbanization wholesale, while another moderate group called for men to take from the west, but to keep the Arab heritage—in other words, to blend oriental and western modes of thought. Then there were those who were conservative, and did not believe in importing from the west. They wished to keep the philosophy and customs of the traditional world and to revive that which had been forgotten or fallen into disuse.

This era of the Palestinian emigration is the longest period of my life, extending over more than thirty years. It began in 1948, and continues to this day at the end of 1978, as I write this chapter of my memories. Only God knows how long this situation of exile will go on. From the start of this period we were living in Beirut, and thus from the point of view of daily life these years can be seen simply as a continuation of our life there. Nothing changed for me during this time, and I continued to work on finishing my book until it was completed in 1954. In April of that same year, my mother left this world—may God have mercy on her!—after suffering a great deal from illnesses and having spent her whole life caring for us and serving the disciples of the *ṭarīqa*.

Extracts From Meetings With Western Scholars

In the late 1950s I became acquainted with the great orientalist and Sufi historian, Dr. Margaret Smith, through her valuable works on Sufism and the Sufi masters. This great scholar had written a book about Rabia al-Adawiyya, and presented to us several writings about Sufism and its masters. In her book she had mentioned in particular our lord Ibrahim ibn al-Adham, the Sufi poet Umar ibn al-Farid, and others. She presented some of their poems as well as some of their spiritual teachings, and offered one of her books to me as a gift. Since I do not know English, I asked some of my brethren in the *ṭarīqa* to translate the book for me.

In the late 1950s the president of the German Institute in Beirut, Dr. Field, came to visit me the first time, and was to come again twice thereafter. We exchanged ideas about Sufism and its role in present-day society. I learned that Dr. Field is one of Germany's great scholars and has published a number of lectures, articles, and books. He presented me with two books printed in the German Institute in Beirut in Arabic; the first about Suhrawardi and the second a book of poetry about the journey through Tripoli of Sidi Shaykh Abd al-Ghani al-Nabulusi (may God be pleased with him!). Dr. Field invited me to visit the library of the German Institute in Beirut which housed precious books, many of which were quite old.

Then in the early 1960s a young man came to Beirut who could not have been more than twenty-five years old. He was pursuing his studies in England, and preparing a thesis to obtain his doctorate. The subject of this thesis was the Shadhili *ṭarīqa* from a historical perspective from the time of our lord Abu al-Hasan al-Shadhili (may God be pleased with him!) up to the present. For this purpose the young man was making rounds of Muslim countries to collect all the information he could find about the Shadhili *ṭarīqa*. He was also conducting research about *ṭarīqas* which were originally Shadhili, but had added to their name that of the Shaykh from whom, or in whose time, the *ṭarīqa* had entered a country or region, such as the Shadhili Darqawi *ṭarīqa*, the Shadhili Wafai *ṭarīqa*, the Shadhili Madani *ṭarīqa*, or the Shadhili Yashruti *ṭarīqa*, and so on. This young man had observed that the litanies and invocation, as well as the Sufi teachings and practices, were identical or nearly identical in all of them. The practices of the Madani *ṭarīqa* or in the Yashruti *ṭarīqa* are just as they were in the time of the Imam Ali abu al-Hasan al-Shadhili, and as they were in the time of Abd al-Salam ibn Mashish (may God sanctify their secrets!).

In the late 1960s Dr. Charis Waddy came to visit Beirut, and during her stay there she visited me three times in my house. I asked her how she knew of my name, and she replied that Dr. Abd al-Majid Makkin, the young man from England, had spoken of me to her. Then she told me that before visiting me she had gone to the American University in Beirut and had read part of my first book, *Journey to the Truth* in the library there, so I offered her a copy of the book. She also told me that she would be delivering a lecture in a worldwide conference which was to be held in Geneva, and that she would like to quote some sections about my childhood from the books. Since that visit, we have been on friendly terms with each other, and exchanged several letters up until the civil war broke out in Lebanon and postal communications were cut off.

I met the great scholar, Father Paul Nwiya, director of the School of Philosophy and Literature in the Jesuit University in Beirut, in the late 1960s. This gentleman is well known throughout universities and learned circles and has written and researched a great deal. He came to visit me in my house and presented me with a copy of the valuable work which he translated from Arabic to French—this is the *Sufi Aphorisms* of Ibn Ata Allah.[50] This work had been translated into languages other than Arabic but it was translated into French for the first time by Father Nwiya. During our talk I learned that he had formerly been a student of the great French orientalist Massignon, who wrote a book about al-Hallaj, in which he defended the latter's position.

In the early 1970s I met Dr. Hossein Nasr while he was teaching in the American University in Beirut; he has published many articles, most of which have been translated into various foreign languages. Moreover, he has written scientific, philosophical, and mystical articles which have been published in major magazines in Japan, Iran, India, and Pakistan, Europe and the U.S. The element which stands out most in the writings of Dr. Nasr is his interest in Sufism and Islamic spirituality. He believes that the essence and spirit of Islam is contained in the Sufi spiritual path and particularly in the doctrine of unity (*tawḥīd*), which therefore means that nothing can exist outside the field of religion. Dr. Nasr came to visit me accompanied by Dr. Ahmad al-Pakistani, professor of Islamic philosophy in the American University of Beirut. Each of these great professors had different inclinations. Dr. Hossein Nasr is a Sufi by nature, whereas Dr. Ahmad al-Pakistani[51] is more influenced by philosophy. Since that first meeting, friendship and affection was felt between us and united us in the service of man according to the pleasure of God and His Messenger.

Another time, in the beginning of the 1970s the telephone rang and the voice on the line said, "This is the American University of Beirut calling. We have here a group of western scholars who would like if possible to visit you tomorrow." "Welcome," I replied, "I will be happy to see them, and shall expect them tomorrow." The following day the honorable scholars visited me. Among them was a great man of learning who had embraced Islam, and followed the Sufi way. He had been given the name Abu Bakr Siraj al-Din. Another of the visitors was a great scholar who had also become a Muslim and followed the Sufi way. He was known as Sidi Ibrahim. This learned man deserves much honor for his translation of the *Bezels of Wisdom* (*Fuṣūṣ al-Ḥikam*) by Shaykh Muhy al-Din ibn Arabi (may God be pleased with him!). I remember that the learned man Abu Bakr took off his shoes when he entered my house, as the righteous Muslims of long ago used to do. After we had sat down and begun to talk, Abu Bakr said to me, "I have read your book *Journey to the Truth* which you gave as a gift to the British Museum Library in London, and it is a precious work. Where did you study? From which university did you graduate?" "I never entered a university, nor even a school," I said. "Then how have you written this book?" he asked. "I wrote it with love and devotion, for I love my father and believe he is my master and guide." Abu Bakr said, "This is the station of the extinction of the disciple in his master. When he is thus extinguished, it is the master who speaks with the tongue of the disciple." I was impressed during this visit by the fact that these honorable foreign scholars spoke the classical Arabic with great proficiency. I explained to them that Muslims should expend great efforts in the fields of science, knowledge, and technology but keep in mind the verse, "Behold what is in the heavens and the earth."[52] The explanation and relevance of this verse is told by our Shaykh Ibn Ata Allah al-Iskandari (may God be pleased with him!) in his *Ḥikam*: "It is permitted for you to contemplate created beings—'Behold what is in the heavens'—the door of inspiration will then open for you. It did not say simply 'Behold the earth' so that you be not guided unto mere physical bodies, for the physical forms are like the shells over the pearls of the archetypes. Whoever stops at the shell is veiled from the beauty of the innermost pearls." This is the explanation of my lord Ibn Ata Allah. Through consideration of this verse and meditation upon its meaning, it becomes clear that we the Muslims are told to regard what is found in the universe of creation and creatures.

One of the greatest and dearest memories for me is that of my meeting with the great scholar, doctor of the law, and devoted Sufi, the honorable Shaykh Abd al-Halim Mahmud, formerly minister of the religious fund and affairs at the Azhar University. One blessed evening in the spring of 1972 the telephone rang. It was the secretary of the bureau of religious affairs in Beirut who introduced himself and said that the minister of religious affairs from Egypt, Doctor Abd al-Halim Mahmud, would like to visit me and wanted to know what time and place would be appropriate. I said, "Welcome to his honor and whoever accompanies him in my humble house tomorrow." "Then we will come tomorrow at eleven," he replied. Thus this great meeting took place in my home. The distinguished visitor was accompanied by a party of religious scholars, both Egyptian and Lebanese, among them the famous reciter of the Quran, Abd al-Basit Abd al-Samad, who delighted us by his recitation of some verses from *Sura Maryam*. After exchanging greetings, I asked our great Shaykh if he was a Sufi who was attached to a *ṭarīqa* or if he was merely a Sufi historian. He replied, "I am a Sufi. My Shaykh is Sayyidna Abu al Hasan al-Shadhili, may God sanctify his secret, and may we benefit by his teachings." During this visit we discussed several important issues, and I remember saying to him, "I consider this visit from you in this humble house not as an honor directed at me personally, but as an honor and a sign of respect to all women following the Sufi path." At one point in our conversation this great visitor asked when I first began to follow the Sufi path, and I replied, "There was no beginning for me, for I was raised in my father's *zāwiya* in a house in which the Name of God was invoked much, and thus in a spiritual ambiance. It was inevitable and natural that I should be a Sufi."

At the beginning of 1973, Dr. Yusuf Ibish came to see me and asked if I would participate in a worldwide conference which was to be held in Houston, Texas. I asked him to excuse me, for I was not able to travel there because of the great distance and my delicate health. Dr. Ibish then had another idea, which was that I participate in the conference with an article on an aspect of Sufism which someone would deliver there on my behalf. I began to prepare the lecture and chose the theme Contemplation and Action—The Sufi Path. When I had finished this article and had it typed I presented it to my friend Dr. Ibish, who read it and appeared pleased with it. He took it from me to translate it into English. The English translation recently appeared in print with all of the articles which were read at the conference in a large volume entitled *Traditional Modes of Contemplation and Action*.[53]

One cold winter night in 1974, I suddenly felt a great pain in my left eye. It was as though a heavy veil had blocked its vision and light. I became afraid, and in spite of the fact that this condition went away the following day, I went to the eye doctor to tell him of this symptom which I had never before experienced. After examining my eye and making tests, they advised me to have an operation on it to remove the glaucoma that was afflicting it, and so the following day I entered the American University hospital in Beirut and requested that my sister Maryam stay with me to help me. I also requested that the doctor tell me when the operation was to be at least an hour beforehand. He asked me why, and I said, "I wish to pray to God, and recite the litanies of the Shadhili Yashruti *ṭarīqa* and devote myself to asking God for help." The doctor said, "Praise be to God! This will no doubt benefit you." When I was being taken to the operating room I entrusted myself to God, saying, "My God! Thou art the guardian of my eye. If Thou will, Thou will grant it light and sight; if Thou will, Thou will extinguish it. Thine is the matter from beginning to end. Do what Thou will with it. Thou art my Master, most merciful of those who show mercy. What happens to me is only by means of Thine instrument, for Thou art my mover." At the end of the operation I heard the doctor's voice say, "Thanks be to God, the operation was successful." After staying in the hospital a few weeks, I returned home and stayed in bed for several more, and my eye regained its sight, thanks be to God.

In the beginning of 1975 great agitation and unrest began to manifest itself among people and in the general climate of life in Lebanon. Then in the beginning of March there was an armed collision between two different factions and this state of unrest, varying between sporadic outbreaks of violence at times and peace at other times, persisted until the summer, when affairs worsened and the fighting intensified. As our house was very close to the center of the trouble, we were compelled to move elsewhere. Once in our new home my sister Maryam's health deteriorated and it became clear that there was no hope for her recovery. She ceased speaking for several days. Then after dawn one day in the beginning of July she spoke and said, "My honored father has come, and with him my mother," and after a few moments she gave up her soul peacefully and quietly. Her departure left such a great pain and sadness in my soul that I cannot describe it in words; following her death the years have passed quickly and painfully, for ever since 1975 we have lived in days of unrest, anxiety, and civil war. God only knows the outcome of it all, glorious and most high is He!

I now lived all alone and traveled between my house and that of my nephew, Shaykh Muhammad al-Hadi, the Shaykh of the Yashruti *ṭarīqa* at present. Whenever the fighting intensified around my house I would collect my things and go to my nephew's house. Then at the end of the summer of 1977, I felt a great need to leave this ambiance torn with strife, and so decided to go to Damascus and stay for some time to rest. Now it was not permitted at the time for Lebanese to leave Lebanon except with official permission from a particular office, and this permission was not easy to obtain, but after great efforts I managed to get a permit to travel to Syria. I went from Beirut to Damascus and then on to the town of Harasta near the capital. I stayed a few months there until the weather became very cold, and then returned to Beirut. In Damascus I had begun to relive the life which I had recently lost. The disciples there refreshed my heart with their Sufi songs and we renewed our meetings of invocation and devotion. I felt then as though I was living in those far off days of my life when I was young.

After returning to Beirut, and living mostly in my nephew's house for nearly one and a half years, I again felt a few weeks ago a great desire to visit Damascus. I made up my mind, and placing my trust in God, traveled there and stayed in houses of the disciples of the *ṭarīqa*. During this recent visit, I became acquainted with a group of great scholars who combined in themselves knowledge of the outward (*sharīʿa*) and inward (*ḥaqīqa*) from the Qadiri, Rifai, Shadhili, and other Orders. In them I found the living spirituality and Sufi brotherhood which unites followers of the path under the banner of the Muhammadan message.

I had come to Damascus this time to visit my brethren in God, the spiritual children of my honored father, and I found them as on my previous visit, devoted and enthusiastic for their religion and their path in spite of the strong movements towards materialism that they were confronted with. If it were not for their firm faith they could not be as they are, and this is no doubt due to God's favor and bounty which He bestowed upon them, and due to His guiding them to the straight path.

The Damascus that I saw in these two recent visits, the new Damascus, is not as I used to know it. Where are the oriental buildings? Where are the beautiful palaces? Where are the homes surrounded by trees, flowers, and water fountains? Whoever walks in the streets of Damascus today finds himself amidst towering buildings, floors upon floors in height, and wide streets overflowing with hundreds, no, thousands of automobiles. It is as though man were witnessing the Last Day there. Entry into the city used to give a feeling of expansiveness, for one would see a river with papyrus, and trees and gardens at times along the right and at times on the left. Now this has been obliterated beneath a roof of cars and vehicles coming and going. This is the nature of the city; artificial beauty replacing natural beauty.

There is no victory or strength save in God! I write these words while in the city of Damascus. Yesterday I had great pains in my chest and experienced such a weakness in my body as I have not felt in all my life. It was as though knives were piercing my breast. Now that I feel better and at peace, I hasten to record these observations, for I know not what God has written for me. I ask Him to accept my worship and to forgive my weakness. He is the Lord of my happiness, and He it is who has charge of my affairs. To Him belong all events and their outcomes, and He has power over all things.

Sufism

It will be necessary for me to write some chapters about Sufism in order to clarify what the requirements are for those who travel on the path and who seek knowledge. I have based my writing on the beliefs and sayings of Sufi masters as expounded in their valuable works. It is no wonder that I rely on these noble guides, for they are shining lights who combine knowledge of the outward and inward, both in its branches and its essences, throughout the realms of principles, *ḥadīth*, exegesis, law, logic, and other sciences. The knowledge of these men encompasses all other realms, both in theory and in application, and is marked by spiritual intuitions, states of ecstasy, and inspirations. Shirani, Suyuti, and a group of Sufi masters have said, "Sufism is no doubt a kind of law, for most of it consists of commands which are obligatory and recommended, as well as containing things that are forbidden and disliked." And they said, "Sufism is the cream of the worshipper's acts—those who are devoid of the weaknesses and whims of the soul, just as the knowledge of meanings and explanations of words is the cream of the science of grammar; it is moreover, its essence and its subtle nature. Thus whoever places the science of Sufism apart from law is correct, and whoever proclaims it to be the essence of law is also correct."[54]

Those who are saints (may God be pleased with them!) are at the same time scholars who practice consensus (*ijtihād*). They do not introduce a new law by this practice but only a new understanding of the law according to the Quran and the practice of the Prophet. Our master Ahmad Zarruq (may God sanctify his secret!) said, "The relation of Sufism to religion is like that of the spirit to the body, for it is the station of excellence (*iḥsān*), which the Messenger of God described to Gabriel. The latter once asked him about it, and he said, 'It is that you worship God as though you saw Him; and if you do not see Him, yet verily He sees you.'"[55] The conditions for entering into this station of excellence are seven: repentance (*tawba*), turning towards God (*ināba*), asceticism (*zuhd*), commitment (*tafwīḍ*), contentment (*riḍa*), sincerity (*ikhlās*), and confidence in God (*tawakkul*). These things are not foreign to Islam, nor are they recent additions to it. The origins of Islamic Sufism are to be found in the Quran, in *ḥadīth*, in Islamic doctrine, and in the laws of the primordial religion. The origin of the name "*fuqarāʾ*" (poor), by which they call themselves and those who enter their path and follow their way, has its precedents in *ḥadīth* and in God's noble Book, where it says, "O mankind! Ye are the poor before God."[56] And He said through the lips of Moses (peace and blessings be upon him!), "My Lord! I am needy (*faqīr*) of whatever good Thou sendest down for me."[57]

There is disagreement about the origin of the words *Ṣufīyya* and *Ṣufī*, but it has been said that the first has been used to denote the noble science and the second to denote he who has realized it. The word *taṣawwuf* is used to refer to the journey and the path and the word *mutaṣawwuf*, to refer to the person who undertakes this journey, but there have been disagreements as to its derivation. It has been said that it comes from the word *ṣūf* (wool), because a Sufi with regard to God is like wool cast in the wind which takes no direction of its own will, and it has been said that it is the quality of one who possesses praiseworthy characteristics and has left behind blameworthy characteristics. Our master Shaykh Taj al-Din ibn Ata Allah al-Iskandari related in his book *Laṭāʾif al-Minan*, on the authority of his Shaykh Abu al-Abbas al-Mursi (may God sanctify his secret!) that the latter said, "The Sufi is the product of what God has done to him, meaning God purifies him and so he is purified (*Ṣafahu Allāhu fa Ṣūfiya*)." And he said, "I also heard him (may God be pleased with him!) say, 'The Sufi is supported by four letters; *Ṣad*, *waw*, *fā*, and *yā*. The *Ṣad* stands for his patience (*ṣabr*), his sincerity (*ṣidq*), and his purity (*ṣafā*). The *waw* is his ecstasy (*wajd*), his love (*wud*), and his loyalty (*wafāʾ*). The *fā* is his bereavement (*faqd*), his poverty (*faqr*), and his extinction (*fanāʾ*). The *yā* denotes a relationship, and is added to him when he is imbued with all of the preceding qualities.'"[58] And Shaykh Muhy al-Din ibn Arabi said, "Sufism means that God purifies you by His marvelous Order, His remarkable Being, and his subtle Essence, and this is granted only to those who watch over their soul, who draw near to God, and who are sincere."[59]

Many wonder why the call to Sufism was not heard in the earliest years of Islam, but only after the time of the Companions and their followers, and they wonder why the Companions themselves were not called Sufis. The answer is that they (may God be pleased with them!) were guided by wisdom of the noble companionship of the Messenger of God (peace and blessings be upon him!) and by their imitation of him, their devotion and piety, their struggle against the ego, and their extinction in their love for God and His Messenger. This honor of companionship and what was associated with it is greater and is preferred over all other titles that could be given them.[60] As for the followers of the Companions, because they were people of worship, striving, and spiritual exercise, they did not need a teaching to guide them to what they already understood. It was only after the era of these noble masters passed that it became necessary to call people to Sufism, for then many began to neglect the path to God, and turned instead towards the world. Forgetfulness took hold of their souls and so the leaders of this science began to call and guide people back to it. These were the circumstances in which it was ordered that its wisdom be recorded so that its nobility would be established. This was a time in which all the different groups of scholars and lawyers set about writing down and recording knowledge of various arts and sciences, and this gave rise to a greater volume of books on these subjects than anywhere else in the world. Ahmad Zarruq said, "When the science of Sufism came to be composed of knowledge and action, acquiring this knowledge from Shaykhs was more beneficial than acquiring it from some other source. 'There are clear signs in the hearts of those who believe.' Thus there was a sign that attached itself to the station of Shaykh, just as the Companions of the Prophet (peace and blessings be upon him!) took the sign from him, and he in his turn took it from Gabriel (peace be upon him!), following his counsel to be a slave of God and a Prophet, and those who came afterwards obtained guidance from the Companions."[61]

Our Sufi masters have agreed that Sufism is wisdom which confers happiness in both worlds through knowledge of the divine. God said, "He unto whom wisdom is given hath truly received abundant good."[62] It is necessary for whoever wishes to attain to something of divine wisdom to educate himself in the essential rules of religious law and the ways of the inward. These are: the guarding of the soul over the thoughts, discerning the true from the false and the praiseworthy from the blameworthy, and the emptying of the heart from the whims and weaknesses of the soul, thereby purifying it. For when the soul is purified and the mirror of the heart is clear, the lights of divine majesty and holy knowledge will be reflected therein. Then the lights of the knowledge of the Essence will radiate, and the springs of divine wisdom will gush forth. Our master Ibn Ata Allah al-Iskandari said in his *Ḥikam*: "Perchance the lights come and find the heart laden with the forms of created things. Then they depart from whence they came. Empty your heart of all else but God; He will then fill it with secrets and lights." Thus liberation from the soul and triumph by knowledge of God are the fruits of purification.

The Sufi masters have said that the science of Sufism is the noblest and most exalted of all sciences without question. This is because its subject is the knowledge of God, blessed and most high through His Names, qualities and actions. A science ennobles through the nobility of that which is known, and through its fruits. Thus the knowledge of God is more noble than knowledge of all else that can be known, for that which belongs to it is the noblest and most perfect of all things knowable and its fruits are the best fruits. This science of the inward revolves on two principles: Knowledge of God and an understanding of His manifestations through His Names, qualities and actions, and knowledge of souls, their stations, perfections, faults, and good qualities and vices. The key to man's realization of God is knowledge of himself, for how can one know his Lord who does not know himself? "He who knows himself knows his Lord."[63] One must understand the reality of this world and the conditions of the hereafter, keep guard over the soul, and prefer the love of God to all else. From the knowledge of the divine springs many branches of knowledge, and all of these can be reduced in their essence to sincerity of devotion. Abu Naim said, "Sincerity of devotion is conditional upon its being such that God is pleased with it, and that which is conditional will not be realized without realizing first its condition." And he said, "There is no Sufism without law, for the outward ordinances of God most high can only be known by means of the latter, and there is no law without Sufism, for there is no true act without sincerity of intention, and neither of these two can in turn be grasped aright without faith. Thus neither the law nor Sufism can be understood apart from each other. They remain inseparable, as the soul is within the body; there is no discrimination between the two except from within (the soul), just as it has no cohesion—meaning in form—except by it (the body)."[64] The Sufi who is realized and who has attained union does not worship for the sake of acquiring merit or for fear of punishment, but rather in order to draw nearer to God, contenting himself with His bountiful countenance and obedience to His order. It is told that the one who realized God, Rabia al-Adawiyya (may God be pleased with her!) used to pray one hundred *rak^cas* (sequence of two prostrations) every night and then address God, mighty and glorious, saying, "Not out of fear of Thy fire or desirous of Thy Paradise, but out of yearning for Thy bounteous countenance." And the Sufi masters have said, "If the realized man speaks, it is in God, if he hears it is through God, if he moves it is by order of God, and if he is quiet he is with God; for he lives in God, for God, and with God."

Imam Suyuti in his book, *Taʾyīd al-ḥaqīqa alʿāliyya bi Tashyīd al-ṭarīqa al-Shādhiliyya*, says on the authority of the author of the *Taʿarruf*[65] that "The Sufis are agreed that God most high is One, Alone, Unique, and Self-Subsisting; Eternal, Knowing, All-Powerful, the One Reality. He is the Hearer, the Seer. The essences of things do not resemble His Essence, nor their qualities His Quality. His act is without cause...there is no ascription to His Essence, nor any effort in His action." He also said, "They are agreed that He, most high, cannot be seen in this world with the eyes or the hearts save through the door of certitude, meaning the certitude of His existence, for this confers the greatest honor and highest blessing upon the slave."[66] Suyuti also related the statement of al-Ghazali in his *Ihyā'* as follows: "When names are applied to God they are not applied with the same fundamental meaning as when applied to a created thing. For example, the name the 'present' (*al-ḥāḍir*), which is shared by all created things, does not signify at one and the same time the Creator and the creation, but rather, everything outside of God that exists and that follows His existence. Now the existence of that which follows after is not equal to that of the one followed; this relationship is comparable to the participation of the plant and the tree in a similar but not equal structure. They are not identical, and this distance exists between all the rest of the divine names and their earthly counterparts, such as knowledge, will, power, and so on."[67]

It may then be asked how it is that some Sufis have said things expressing their direct vision of God, as in the words of Umar ibn al-Farid, "If I ask Thee to see Thee in Thy Reality, permit it! Do not make the answer 'Thou shall not see.'" The answer to this is in the explanation of my lord Shaykh Ala al-Din al-Qunawi, one of the Shafii imams, in his book *Sharḥ al-Taᶜarruf*, which Suyuti quoted in his *Taʾyīd*, as follows: "He said, 'This can be explained by several things; the first is that the expression of subtle truths that are experienced while in a state of ecstatic love for God is very difficult, because of the nature of this state. Do you not see that a man who wants to describe the sweetness of sugar cane to one who has never tasted it by using words that try to convey its reality in a way that the listener will grasp, will never be able to? And he said, One who has realized God may have a subtle truth in his heart he wishes to express but is unable to put into words, and he may then receive an inspired means of expression, as al-Ghazali said concerning the station of extinction in God: The doctors of the outward law are incapable of explaining this state by using words that are clear and that convey the idea so that it is understood. The author of the *Taᶜarruf*[68] said, It is not possible to express the perceptions of hearts and innermost beings in their full reality by words; rather they are known through assiduous searchings, and ecstatic love, and none will realize God except he who has come into direct contact with these states.'"[69]

The word "union" (*ittiḥād*) as used by Sufis means to surrender affairs to God, to give up one's will to Him, and to surrender one's preference and course of action to His divine order without opposition. It is to leave behind all of creation and the power of giving to it and withholding from it. Abu Ayyub said, "For he who is free of works, those which he did not know he possessed will be written for him. There is no enemy to corrupt him, nor ego to be pleased thereby." The author of the *Ta^c^arruf* said, "The meaning of this is that the servant cuts himself off from the world and returns to God, divorced from all his acts." And al-Qunawi said, "When the servant has perfected his devotion to God and has extinguished himself so that he is no longer aware of his actions, his act then becomes as though it were not his own; it is as though he did nothing—it is not written among his deeds, and the enemy does not corrupt it, nor does the soul take pleasure in it...." Moreover, what they ascribe to themselves that can only be ascribed to God most high is as something done by God; an example is the *ḥadīth* of al-Bukhari, transmitted by Abu Hurayra (may God be pleased with him!) which tells that the Prophet (peace and blessings be upon him!) said, "The reward for My believing slave when I have taken his pure soul from among the inhabitants of the earth and credited him with it, is Paradise." He said this speaking with the mouth of his Lord. And he said, "There is not one of us but he has a station known by God."[70] This was said by the angel through him.

In the words of Suyuti, "Al-Hafiz ibn Hajar said, 'Some of the later Sufis have said of the station of extinction and effacement that it is the ultimate goal. It means to be present through the presence of God in the disciple, to love with His love for him, to see through His gazing at him so that nothing worthy of a name remains with him, and it means not to stop at a form or become attached to a thing or be described as something. He must bear witness to the manifestation of the Truth in him, so that he himself manifests it, and must bear witness to God's love for him so that he loves Him, and bear witness to His looking at His slave until he draws near, looking back at Him with the eye of the heart.' There can be nothing obscure in this explanation."[71]

I close this chapter with the words of Shaykh Ahmad Zarruq (may God sanctify his secret!) from his book *Qawāᶜid al-Taṣawwuf*: "One must realize the fundamental precepts of the religion and carry them out according to the rules of the rightly-guided Imams, for the Sufi school comes after the schools of the first believers. The divisions of belief are three; first, that which is believed in respect to Lordship; in this there is only the negation of the possibility of attributes to God and of His immanence. The second is that of the plane of Prophethood and this is none other than its affirmation and its exaltation over all knowledge, deeds, and states, which in its perfection does not permit any deficiency. It is for the lord to say what he wills to his servant and it is for the servant to take upon himself what his master wishes, in humility to him. Our duty is to educate ourselves in the attitude of the servant and to realize the extent of his relationship with God.[72] Thirdly, the belief in the hereafter, and that all things are governed by the Sovereign Good, and this is none other than sincere faith."[73]

The Path

What is meant here by "the path" is the path which leads to God; it is the way of the Sufi masters. It has outward and inward aspects; the first of these is related to the improvement of outward duties, and the second is related to the improvement of the inner depths of man. The people who travel upon this special path must have perfect understanding of the doctrine and watch over their souls in order to be united to Him while working and while at rest, with every breath and in every moment, so that the divine presence becomes fixed in the heart, and the latter is given peace from worldly states and vicissitudes. Al-Ghazali, in speaking of the stations of the path being in the essence of the

Quran, said: "The Quran has six intentions, and the sixth one is to give instruction about the levels of the path. This is alluded to in the opening chapter where it says, 'Thee (alone) do we worship and Thee (alone) we ask for help.'"[74] And al-Tibi said in his *Ḥāshiat al-Kashshāf*, "There are four sciences pertaining to religion, and each of them is contained in the opening chapter. They are the science of origins, the science of the branches of knowledge, the science of stories, and the science by which one attains to perfection. This last is the science of human virtues and its greatest possibility is fulfilled when one attains the Eternal Presence and takes refuge in the Unique Reality, following the way of the Prophet. There is an allusion to this in God's words, 'And Thee alone we ask for help—guide us on the straight path.'[75] Furthermore, it can be deduced by allusion from the rest of the chapter that there are many other paths that do not practice the ways of the Prophet; let them be warned—those are of the path 'With whom God is angry and who go astray.'[76] Here I end."

The Sufi masters have agreed that Sufism does not consist in reading works written about it, but in striving to cleanse the heart and purify it of noxious diseases; to correct the soul and to put a stop to its shameful deeds and restore it to its original essence, as in the words of God: "O thou soul at peace! Return to thy Lord, content and in His pleasure."[77] No matter how numerous and diverse the paths are, they can all be reduced in the end to knowledge and realization. Our master and Shaykh Ahmad Zarruq (may God be pleased with him!) said in his *Qawāᶜid*, "The many aspects of the good give rise to the many ways of realizing it; and thus there is a different path for each group. For the generality there is a Sufism which is contained in the works of Muhasibi[78] and others like him. For the lawyer there is a

Sufism which Ibn al-Hajj[79] in his *Madkhāl* has elaborated. For the *ḥadīth* scholar there is a Sufism which Ibn Arabi deals with in his *Sirāj*. For the worshipper there is a Sufism which al-Ghazali speaks of in his *Minhāj*. For the one who concentrates on acts of worship there is a Sufism which al-Qushayri in his *Risāla* outlines. For the recluse there is a Sufism which the *Iḥyā'*[80] and the *Qūt*[81] tell of. For the learned man there is a Sufism which al-Hatimi[82] included in his books. For the logician there is a Sufism which Ibn Sabin[83] speaks of in his works. For the naturalist there is a Sufism expounded by al-Biruni[84] in his *Asrār*, and for principialists there is a Sufism which al-Shadhili showed by his realization. Thus let each one consider from where he should start out, based on his own nature."[85]

The greatest secret with respect to the path of the will (*irāda*) is in His words, glory be to Him! "Those who hear advice and follow the best thereof. Such are those whom God hath guided and such are men of understanding."[86] Shaykh Abu Bakr al-Tamistani[87] spoke of the path thus, "The path is clear, and we have the Book and practice of the Prophet behind us; the grace bestowed on the companions is shown by their having been first to emigrate for God, and by their companionship to the Prophet. Thus whoever makes the Book and the practice of the Prophet his companion, detaches himself from the world and from his ego, and emigrates for God in his heart, that one is of the truly sincere."[88] My lord Shaykh Ibn Abbad al-Shadhili (may God be pleased with him!) divides the path into two parts and those who follow them into two groups; the first group includes those on the paths of polishing the heart and illuminations. It is the path that makes use of spiritual exercises and endeavors to cleanse the character. The second group includes those who follow the path of inquiry and devotion to knowledge combined with striving to cleanse the heart and master the lower soul. In addition, one of the Poles of the Shadhili *ṭarīqa* related what our master Ahmad Zarruq said on this in the *Mabāḥith al-Aṣliyya*, and I thought to transmit this passage in its entirety in my book on account of its usefulness for disciples on the path. Concerning the first group, he said, "The soul, when it first comes to life is like a clean, polished mirror in which everything that comes to it from the past and future is clearly reflected. But then it becomes obstructed in men by one of two things: either it becomes rusted by contemplating, trusting, and supporting itself on images of forms, or, it loses sight of its original function and occupies itself with various types of knowledge, deeds, and other things which become imprinted in the heart and cause it to depart from its original purpose. If in the first case the heart-mirror is polished it will surely see the truth, for the fog will have been cleansed. And if in the second case the heart-mirror turns in devotion it will perceive the truth because its veil has been negated. But as long as it is rusted or has turned away, it is existing apart from what is intended for it and it will be impossible for it to regain its function. For this reason it is said in the *Ḥikam*[89] 'How can the heart be illumined when the forms of created things are imprinted on its mirror? How can it travel to God when it is shackled by its desires? How can it desire to enter into the presence of God while it is not cleansed of its forgetfulness? How can it hope to understand the subtle aspects of mysteries when it has not yet repented of its wrongdoings?' Just as this first group likens the soul to a mirror, so they also compare it to a spring of water and liken the knowledge and realization in the soul to that which is within the spring, saying, 'The spring has become dry and only by digging will the water gush forth once more.'

This similitude of the soul to the spring is true, for the soul has become distracted by illusions and accidents from the divine realities and knowledge which shone upon it at the time of its original pact with God. Thus the truth seeped away from it, like water that trickles away from a dry spring, so that one must dig down with the hoe of effort and the shovel of spiritual exercise until it gushes forth as much as before, or even more so. This group are on the path which seeks to polish the heart and they are called the illuminationists. They hold that the most fundamental cure—that is, for the malady of the soul—will be the most effective means of curing the whole person. For by cutting the disease off at its root, the branches are also cut off, unlike the one who treats a branch by itself—this treatment cannot cure, the patient will not be restored to health until the true cause of the malady is known. If the cause and origin of the malady have not been understood, then their annihilation will not permanently benefit the person. Even if the treatment benefits at first, its recovery will either be impeded by this lack of understanding, or it will be in the wrong proportions and will ultimately fail. Therefore, know the cause of your disease, so that you might be successful in curing it in the shortest possible time and with the most suitable treatment. Only then will you be safe from later disturbances.

"The origin of every physical complaint lies in the weakness of the physical constitution, which leads it to have abnormal actions and reactions, and the origin of every malady of the heart lies solely in corrupt intentions, marked by contentment with the ego, so that its actions and reactions take place outside the realm of the law and the truth, and even go so far as to conform to false desires and tendencies that spring from lack of certitude and self-indulgence. To cure the soul it is necessary to hold it back from its tendencies to faults and forgetfulness until it is no longer subject to them, and to purify it until it is free of all of this through piety and good works, and until these last are all that remain in it. This is first, and second, one must purify it through repentance and turning to the straight path so that it takes on the qualities of righteousness, piety, and so on. This is the path of illumination and polishing of the heart, which is so ancient that it existed even before the law; for it consists only in polishing the mirror of the heart and nothing more. It will continue to exist for as long as time endures and will never pass away, although there are times when it will be carried out by the practice of spiritual retreats, regular worship, and the like, and times when it will be through keeping only to the fundamental rites of the religion, and times when it will be through preserving the sacred rites and nothing more, and times when it will be through utter devotion to learning and the company of spiritual men. These things endure forever, in spite of the fact that the practice of spiritual retreats has all but disappeared nowadays. Some of our masters have said, 'Striving for perfection by means of such practice ceased in the year 824 A.H.[90] and naught remains of it but our devoted and fervent memory of it.' It is therefore your duty to follow the practices of the Prophet, neither being excessive nor falling short of them; in other words, follow them with earnest adherence and with sincerity of intention, and with God is our victory.

"Another group includes the people of the path of inquiry and devotion to learning. These have said that to take hold of the truth from the outside is superior; they make use of the pursuit of knowledge in their path, for a door is of no use without its key. Thus they treat the soul by means of their knowledge and consequent action, for through this practice the lights within the soul respond to those that come to it from without and by their brilliance they abolish the darkness within at its root and throughout its branches. This path is the best one to follow to attain perfection, because the goal of the first one is to attain to perfection of soul and no more, whereas the goal of this last is the attainment of wisdom along with perfection of the soul, and this is the highest purpose. This group declares that knowledge is the key to action, in accordance with his words (may God bless him and give him peace!): 'Knowledge takes precedence over works, for they come after it. Whosoever seeks the good will obtain it, whosoever fears evil will be protected from it, and whosoever acts by what he knows, God will grant him knowledge of that of which he is ignorant.'[91]

"One must study four fields of knowledge: that of the Essence and attributes of God, that of religious law, that of exegesis and traditions of the Prophet, and that of states and stations. Knowledge of the Essence and attributes signifies knowledge of the unity of God (*tawḥīd*). This knowledge is acquired through learning the doctrine of a master such as Imam Abu Hamid al-Ghazali and by understanding its proofs in whatever way one is capable without subjecting them to similitudes. One must see in them reflections from the holy Book and the practice of the Prophet, the realities of existence and so on, and in time, by making this the focal point of one's efforts, its reality will color the aspirant and cause him to attain to the station of certitude, and he who has certitude discovers its sweetness. When one has attained to this level it abides in the soul to the extent that it has been ordained to receive it, and thus to journey on the path in a blessed manner and in pure devotion. We have no need to describe this last aspect.

"As for knowledge of religious law, the way to learn it is to study with one who is considered to be a leader in this field in his time, and to pursue his representations of it without going into excess, until he has assimilated all of the chapters and has fixed them in his mind without excess, for excess causes dispersion of the mind—when he has realized these truths, he looks upon existence and upon things and can easily give explanations and judgments about them. Whoever knows the nature of existence—that is, its aspects and God's actions within it, through efforts and realization (for the one depends on the other)—experiences the ascent of the light within his heart, which brings him exaltation and honor. This light makes the heart participate only in knowledge and not in what does not concern it, and it is no longer limited to questions or doubts that can cause the heart to be divided, particularly in one who lacks fervor.

"Knowledge of *ḥadīth* signifies an understanding of its principles, not knowledge of the manner and means of its transmission, and this in turn calls for knowledge of exegesis. It is through these two that the divine lights of wisdom shine upon the first two realms of knowledge, although whoever pursues his study of law to the end will also be given wisdom and authority as long as he does not depart from the precepts of the Imams, but makes them his poles of reference. It was said, 'Stop in your study where the Imams stopped, then give your interpretation.' He who takes his interpretation from the texts of the holy Book and the practices of the Prophet speaks truly if he bases himself thus, and if not, then the words of one who knows not are to be shamed. Whosoever fails to emulate the wise fails to be guided. For this reason there is no religious leader who ignores the statements of the first leaders of Islam—rather, he follows in their footsteps. He who confuses the Quran and the *Sunna* and the law concerning them should realize what we have said. This point was presented by Shaykh Abu Abd Allah Ibn Abbad in his treatises where he spoke of innovation and tradition, and with God is the victory."

Knowledge of stations and states and the mode of conduct and behavior in them is what the Sufis are most concerned about. There are two paths regarding this: one concerns the vision of God from the greatest proximity and the works associated with this that serve to nourish it. This is the Shadhili path and that of those of similar tendencies. The path of the vision of the soul, the guardianship of God over it and the works associated with it constitute the path of al-Ghazali and whoever follows his way. This way is based upon the *ḥadīth* which says that you should "worship God as if you saw Him"—this corresponds to the Shadhili path, "and if you do not see Him, yet verily He sees you"—this corresponds to the path of al-Ghazali.

The Shadhili *ṭarīqa* is among the most complete of the Sufi paths, for it combines knowledge, works, devotion, and love. It is the path of clear proofs, those attached to it are those who seek and devote themselves to knowledge and realization. Being comprised of receptivity to the divine attraction while in a state of perfect sobriety and striving, it encompasses the various modes of comportment, reverence, and submission, and is built upon knowledge of the outward and inward. Thus no state of divine ecstasy can lead to exceeding the bounds of right conduct, nor can a state of sobriety lead to a decrease in intimacy or to being veiled from the divine. It is a marriage of perfect qualities of the outward law and inner essence. It has kept itself balanced and within the limits of moderation by the grace of God, and has gained victory by this last quality through His guidance. It is founded upon unitive consciousness of God through the attitude of worship and contemplation of Him without creating fissures in oneself and by performing the duty of spiritual retreats and the invocation of His Name according to the tenets of the *ṭarīqa*. Shaykh Mahmud Abu al-Shamat al-Dimashqi mentioned in his explanation of the litany the following: "Abu al-Hasan said, 'I asked my Lord that the Pole of the age be from my lineage until the end of time, and I heard the call, "O Ali, I have answered your request."'" Our Shaykh and Imam Ali Abu al-Hasan al-Shadhili did not enter upon the path until he had taken part in discussions of the outward sciences. He was thus very knowledgeable about the fine points of these realms of learning. He (may God be pleased with him!) was born in the village of Ghamara in North Africa near Sabtah (Ceuta) in Morocco in the year 1196. He received the Shadhili *ṭarīqa* and inherited the function of Pole of the age from his Shaykh, the Imam Abu Abd Allah Abd al-Salam ibn Mashish (may God sanctify his secret!). Upon receiving the initiation his Shaykh ordered him to travel to a town called Shadhila near Tunis and it was there that he began to be known. Later he moved to Tunis and from there to the more eastern lands. He made the pilgrimage many times and died on the way to Mecca in the year 1258. He was buried near the shore of the Red Sea in the village of Humaythara, in Egypt, and to this day people from all regions and corners of the earth make pilgrimage to his tomb.

The Muhammadan Reality

The Muhammadan Reality is the Light of Muhammad and the first ray of manifestation issuing from God. The *ḥadīth* related by Jabir ibn Abd Allah al-Ansari tells that when he asked the Prophet concerning the first thing that God created, he answered, saying, "The first thing God created was my Light. And from my Light He created all other things." And the Imam Hafiz al-Kabir ibn Hajar was asked in his legal opinions on *ḥadīth* about whether all the angels were created at one time. He replied, "Abd al-Razzaq said on the authority of Jabir ibn Abd Allah al-Ansari that the latter said, 'I said, O Messenger of God, you who are as my father and mother, tell me about the first thing God created before all else.' He replied, 'O Jabir! Before all things, God created the Light of your Prophet Muhammad from His Light. This Light began to spin with the power God had willed for it, and at that time there existed neither the Tablet, nor the Pen, nor Paradise nor Hell, nor the sensible world (*mulk*), nor heaven or earth, sun or moon, man or jinn. When God willed to create beings, He divided this Light into four parts. The Pen was created from the first part, the Tablet from the second, and the Throne from the third. Then He split the fourth into four parts again, and created from the first part the support of the Throne, and from the second its Seat. From the third He created the rest of the angels. Then He divided the fourth section into four smaller ones, and created the heavens from the first, the earths from the second, and from the third, Paradise and Hell. Then He divided the fourth part into three. He created the Light by which believers perceive Him from the first part, and from the second, the Light of their hearts, which is realization (*maᶜrifa*), and from the third part the Light of their souls which corresponds to the testimony of unity (*tawḥīd*)—"There is no divinity save God, Muhammad is the Messenger of God."'"

Our Prophet Muhammad (peace and blessings be upon him!) is the source of all mercy, and the origin of all outward and inward lights. His essence combines in it all other perfect essences. The Prophethood and the Message emanated from his essence (upon him be blessings and peace!), sanctity emanated from his person, and the hearts of his saints and the springs of mercy flow from him throughout all time and in all places. He is the greatest veil; he is the life of the world of the spirit—he who attains to his noble presence has without doubt also attained to the presence of his Lord. God, glorious and most high, made the Muhammadan Reality encompass all of His creation. On account of his pure, pristine essence, the Word of God brought about the creation of all things. For he, God bless him and give him peace, is the first and has been in existence before all else. He is the Seal of the Prophets and has said, "I was a Prophet when Adam was still between spirit and body."

My father has spoken about the Muhammadan Light in these words: "God took a handful of His Light which was the Muhammadan Reality, and it emanated in the form of mercy. From it was made all that was and all that is to be." And he commented on the statement of some Sufi masters to the effect that the presence of Muhammad is in every particle and grain of existence, saying, "This refers to the Muhammadan essence (*sirr*), for the creation would not have been established originally were it not for him; he is the source of everything in existence."

The Sufi masters are agreed that the inheritors of the Prophet who follow the path are of different kinds; among them are the perfect, and the most perfect; those who journey to the Essence by the Essence, and those who journey through the Names and qualities of God. Our lord and greatest Shaykh Abu al-Hasan al-Shadhili said (may God sanctify his secret!): "There is no prophet or Messenger without an heir in this community, and each one is given his inheritance from his legator. The Prophet said, 'The scholars are the heirs of the prophets.' The heir must have a known share in his inheritance, and undertake what his station demands for the sake of the legacy of knowledge and wisdom, and not for the sake of attaining to stations and states, for the stations of the prophets are too exalted for anyone else to be able to perceive their reality." And he said, "Those who imitate the qualities of the prophets are the righteous. Those who imitate those of the Messengers are the sincere. Between the righteous and the sincere there is difference in station, just as there is between the prophets and the Messengers (God bless and give them peace!)." He also said, "Although there is a group who is singled out for sharing the substance of the Messenger of God ... every prophet and saint participates in the substance of the Messenger of God."[92] Here I will add that the meaning behind the words of our Shaykh and master Abu al-Hasan, to the effect that every prophet and saint is of the substance of the Messenger of God, is that they are extensions of the Light of the Muhammadan Reality, which is the origin of all that was and all that will be. My father had a clear and detailed explanation of the nature of these perfected souls, and spoke of them in many of his talks and directives to the disciples of the noble *ṭarīqa*. During one of these lectures, he said: "There are seven who are virtuous in their love for the Prophet, and there is one who is the Pole and guide. When the Pole leaves this world to join his Lord, the seven representatives gather together to select one of their group to be the guide. They often try to flee from this burden and select a saintly disciple as a replacement instead of the one who was destined to be the guide. If their opinions differ as to what the decision should be, they seek refuge in the Messenger of God, going to him and standing before him. Then he chooses one of the representatives. This Pole and guide is the recipient of the Light of the supreme Name of God (*Allāh*), which is superior to all His other Names. He who is illumined by it has all of manifestation submitted to him and moves freely in the sensible and angelic worlds by its authority. He is a guide aided by the spirit of Muhammad."

Sufi Miracles

Miracles in Sufism are a kind of rupture of the normal course of things that God makes manifest through His saints to honor them and as a support to the disciple striving in God's path. A miracle may be manifest either through the speech, deeds, or movements of the saint. They are in no way prophetic miracles (*muʿjizāt*) although they resemble them in their effect and scope.

Prophetic miracles are manifestations above the human level that God wills through His prophets. The greatest of these came to our Messenger Muhammad in the form of the holy Quran—the miraculous Book that God most high sent down to him, the unlettered Prophet, who knew nothing of reading and writing and was ignorant of the science of language, both of its principles and its applications. There have been many miracles performed by the prophets. As we are not going to go into this subject in depth, what I have written here will be sufficient to indicate that the rupture of normal conditions is something possible by the will of God.

The lesser miracles (*karamāt*) are those interruptions of normal existence that God has permitted to be manifested through His saints. God, glorious and most high, is impervious to change and eternal. In the same way, the Light of His Reality cannot die or be extinguished. Saints are the means by which the divine Light radiates to mankind after the appearance of the Prophet Muhammad and after his

Companions. Events that break the normal laws of nature and manifest themselves by God's will through saints are called miracles, for the saints are at the feet of the prophets and the Sufis hold that they do not bring a new revelation but rather undertake to make revelation accessible to people by their profound and enlightened understanding of it. With their guidance, the behavior of men may come to be in conformity with the laws of revelation, for its only reason for existing is to set right societies and all of mankind.

Here I think it is useful to relate a miracle which God performed through one of the greatest Sufis, Shaykh Muhy al-Din ibn Arabi, upon his encounter with a philosopher. Let us read of this miracle as the Shaykh himself tells it. He said: "In the year 586,[93] a philosopher came to us who denied prophethood to the same degree as the Muslims affirm it, and denied miracles that came to the prophets, saying that such things cannot be taken as physical realities. Now the weather at that time was wintry and cold, and we were sitting in front of a coal burner. The deceitful denier said, 'Everyone says that Abraham was thrown into the fire and was not burned, but felt only coolness and peace. But fire by its nature burns combustible bodies. The fire mentioned in the Quran in the story of Abraham was a reference to the raging anger of Nimrod; it was a fire of anger.' When he had finished speaking one of those present (meaning Shaykh Muhy al-Din) said, 'What if I show you that God spoke truly in His literal expression that the fire would not burn Abraham, and that God caused it to be, as He said, coolness and peace, by taking the place of Abraham myself in order to defend him?' 'This is impossible,' the denier said. 'Then see for yourself,' and he threw the hot coals from the burner onto his lap. They stayed on his clothes, and he picked them up with his hands. When the man saw they did not burn him he was astonished. Then the Shaykh put them back in the burner, and said, 'Put your hand near them, now.' So the man stretched out his hand and it was burned. The Shaykh said, 'Thus it was and is yet by command; it burns by divine command or does not by the same. God most high does what He wills.' The denier then submitted and recognized the truth."

When speaking of Sufi miracles I must include for the respected reader some which God manifested through my honored father. Among these is the following: Two weeks after the death of my father the room in which he slept and sat in prayer was closed up and left as it had been during his life. No one entered it except to recite the Quran. Now I was with a young girl at that time who was in retreat at the *zāwiya* and she suggested that we go in to my father's room. So we entered and I sat down where I used to sit during his life, forgetting that he had passed away several days before. After we had stayed there for a few minutes, we saw him sitting on his bed, looking at us and smiling and indicating to us by a movement of his hand that there was no harm in our sitting there in the room. Several minutes passed before my friend, who was older than me, suddenly remembered that my father was already in the next world, yet here we were seeing him with our own eyes! How could this be? The moment she voiced her thought to me his image disappeared, and we began to cry. We left the room full of awe and amazement and everyone came to ask what had happened to us. We could only respond, "Our master was with us in the room."

There is another incident that happened to Shaykh Abd al-Qadir al-Hamsi al-Dimashqi, the Sufi poet of whom my father said, "He is the poet of the *ṭarīqa* in our time." One day Shaykh Abd al-Qadir was sitting before my father in the *zāwiya.* My father spoke to him concerning his achievements in the art of poetry and asked him how he was able to compose poetry so easily and to set it to a melody. He answered, "It is because I am learned in song, harmony, and prosody." At this, my father called to Abu Said al-Qadi, saying, "Close the window behind Shaykh Abduh, and draw the curtains, for he is cold." And from that day on, all inspiration was cut off from Shaykh Abd al-Qadir and remained thus for some time after his return to Damascus. He was unable to compose any poetry, songs, or chanted verses, as he used to do. He was torn with remorse, for he realized he had acted improperly with his Shaykh by claiming abilities for himself while neglecting to say that what he possessed came to him by the grace of God. He repented and decided to return to his Shaykh to ask his pardon, and resolved to change his conduct for one that was worthy of a person on the path. He set off from Damascus to Acre and, arriving at the *zāwiya*, pleaded that the gates be opened to him and the inner curtains raised for him. Because of the sincerity of his state his pleas and requests were answered, and God showed mercy to him once again.

Before the existence of the train, automobile, airplane, the atomic bomb, or petroleum, my father made references to these things through metaphorical expressions. During one of his sessions he addressed those present, saying, "Tomorrow one of you will be in Haifa or Acre and will travel to Syria in one day." At another time he said, "Tomorrow gold will appear from beneath the earth, and will say to the believers, 'Take me,' but the believer will say, 'I do not need you.'" At a third meeting he said, "Nations manufacture explosives, but God, be He glorified, will destroy the world in five minutes." My father spoke of what was revealed to him by the wisdom of his great sanctity and by divine permission. He spoke of the future in metaphors, by allusions or by clear explanations, in accordance with the divine illumination which possessed him at the time.

There is another miracle I wish to record here: Ali Rida Pasha was the secretary during the Caliphate of the Sultan Abd al-Hamid the second. One day the Sultan called him and dictated a letter to him, ordering him to copy it down. To the surprise of the Sultan, Ali Rida Pasha was so awed by the former that he forgot to record some parts of the letter dictated to him. He spent that night in anxiety and fear, waiting to see what would become of him, and resolved to seek refuge in God, petitioning Him and seeking protection in the prophets, saints, and realized souls. While in this state, he heard a voice ordering him to write, and dictating to him what the Sultan had said. He wrote it, although he found a sentence in the letter that the Sultan had not said but which the voice had dictated. This sentence was a legal judgment, so he included it. He found himself asking the voice that had dictated to him who he was, and it replied, "I am the realized soul in whom you sought protection." Ali Rida Pasha asked, "What is your name?" The voice answered "Shaykh Ali Nur al-Din al-Yashruti al-Hasani al-Shadhili, in Acre." Ali Rida said, "Permit me, my lord, to recite the litanies of the Shadhili *ṭarīqa*." The voice permitted him and taught them to him. Ali Rida Pasha thus began using them without having ever met our Shaykh. The following morning he took the papers which he had written to the palace and presented them to the Sultan. The latter was astonished, particularly by the sentence which he had not dictated to him in their previous meeting, and asked how he had known to write it. Ali Rida replied, "A voice dictated it to me." The Sultan said, "What voice is this?" Ali Rida told him the story of what he had heard during the night. The Sultan was amazed and said, "Give me permission to recite what the Shaykh has given you of the litanies of the Shadhili *ṭarīqa*." And so he did.

Here I would like to mention to the generous reader an event that took place before my eyes when I was young. This was the death of our brother in the path, Abd al-Rahman al-Aqil. He was among the pious disciples of my father. Since his youth he used to sing in the Yashruti *zāwiya* in Acre, for God had blessed him with a beautiful and harmonious voice. In spite of his position as president of the city council and the abundance of his official and social duties, he continued to sing regularly in these sessions. Then at one point he fell seriously ill, and very soon after that he passed away to the mercy of God. People hastened to his house, for he was beloved by all. They brought the best doctor in Acre and after examining him he announced that he was indeed in the next world. He gave the death certificate to his family and offered them his condolences. News of this traveled to the *zāwiya* and the disciples hastened to the bereft house. When my father heard the news, he also set off for the departed one's home along with some disciples. By this time this disciple had passed away some hours before and his family had brought someone to wash the body in the ritual manner. Just as they were about to remove his clothing to wash him and prepare him for burial, my father arrived. I was very young at that time, and went with Hajj Salim Baliq, who took care of me, to see what had happened. And there what did I see! My father entered the room in which the corpse of Abd al-Rahman lay, and found the doctor who had treated him and supervised his medications there, along with some notables and officials of the city and others who had come to bid farewell to the one who had left for his final abode.

God had destined for me to witness with my own eyes the miracle which He manifested through my father before all those present. My father stood over the head of Abd al-Rahman, put his mouth to his ear and pronounced the supreme Name of God three times, saying "*Allāh*, *Allāh*, *Allāh*." Then he called him by his name saying, "O Abd al-Rahman." There was no answer. He repeated this another time and there was no answer. The third time we all heard the voice of Abd Al-Rahman say slowly, "*Allāh*." The voice grew louder and louder until it was clear that its origin was truly the body lying prostrate. Then Abd al-Rahman sat up, turned to look around him, and said to my father in astonishment, "Why did you bring me back?" Then, after he had calmed himself a little, he looked at my father, and the latter said to him, "Vision of the naked Essence comes not before penetrating the veils of obscurity" (*astār al-Ghawāshi*). This was a song the words of which are from our lord, Shaykh Ali Wafa, one of the Poles in the chain of the Shadhili *ṭarīqa*. Abd al-Rahman, who had lain down again then began to sing this song with his beautiful voice and it was as though he were no longer ill and had never passed away. My father was still standing over his head saying loudly, "*Allāh*, *Allāh*." Then he motioned to the disciples who were present and they made a circle around the bed of Abd al-Rahman and invoked the Name of God while he sang to the end of the song. The session came to an end with the recitation of ten verses from the holy Quran. Our brother Abd al-Rahman lived for a few weeks following this, then passed on to the next world. This miracle is well known to many from Acre who lived there at that time, some of whom are still alive today.

The Essence of Man

According to the Sufi, the essence of man is that subtle consciousness of the divine rooted within the heart. It is what distinguishes the human being from the animal, and is called the conscious soul (*al-nafs al-nātiqa*). It has been described by the words "soul," "spirit," "heart," "intellect," and "secret," (*al-nafs, al-rūḥ, al-ᶜaql, al-sirr*). The essence of these names is one and the same, and its variation is because of different qualities, for example, if it tends towards faults or defects, it is the soul, and if it tends towards perfection, it is the spirit and heart and intellect. If it becomes empty and is purified and gains control over the means of perfection by leaving behind all trace of defects, it is the secret; at that moment it holds within itself all realities and divine Lights shine forth from the heart of him who possesses it. Shaykh Ibn Ajiba in his book *Sharḥ al-Mubāḥith al-Aṣliyya* said concerning this: "When the soul is purified of the tarnish on its mirror, of complacency with its spiritual station, of distractions, and of miracles, it is then one with the Secret of secrets." He also said, "Know that the progress of the spirit from the soul, and the intellect, heart, and secret all have limits as to the degree of knowledge and realization they can attain. The boundary of knowledge of the soul is the embellishment of the most outward existence. It can be deceived by outward enjoyment and forget the inward, preoccupying itself with pleasures. As for the intelligence, the limit of its knowledge and realization is devotion to its Creator, the abandonment of alterities, and the search for lights, for then it has freed itself from its hobble, and can intensify its search for its erring master. The limit of knowledge of the spirit is its encounter with the lights of the angelic world and its search for the secrets of the archangelic world. It has rested itself from the weariness of the journey, but has not yet attained to the secret. The limit of knowledge and realization of the secret is in the archangelic world, and is attained when the eye of the heart has penetrated there from the station of the angelic world. This is the final goal of the secret. God has said, 'And that thy Lord, He is the Goal.'"[94]

Some people think that Sufism is no more than withdrawal and isolation from the world. This is clearly a great error. What is required of him whom God has favored by this spiritual relationship is that he be an example to the rest of creation by his actions, worship, spirituality, and the correction of his soul and his devotion. He must live among people and work both for his spiritual and worldly life. Shibli (may God be pleased with him!) said, "I read four thousand *ḥadīths*. Then I took one from among them and lived by it, setting aside all others; for I contemplated it and found my liberation and salvation in it. It is as though the knowledge of the first and the last were embodied therein, and I have contented myself to follow it. It is this: "The Messenger of God said, 'Work for this world to the extent that you now exist in it; work for the next world to the extent that your eternal abode is in it; work for God to the degree that you need Him, and work for the Fire to the degree that you must keep away from it.'"

My father followed in the footsteps of his ancestor the Prophet by his attitude of slavehood to God and by worship, obedience, and good works. The disciples of the Shadhili Yashruti *ṭarīqa* in Acre were educated after this model in the time of my father. It was a place for undertaking religious prescriptions, learning outer and inner knowledge, and was a fortress for vigil, contemplation, and absorption in the greatness of God. This life with its various practices was a spiritual one which embodied worship, love of God, and invocation of His Name at all times and in all circumstances.

The Station of Love of the Sufis

The meaning of the word "station" for the Sufis is the position of the servant before God and is the sum of his acts of worship, efforts, and devotion to God. A difference between a "state" (*ḥāl*) and a "station" (*maqām*) exists because the former results from a grace which descends upon the heart but does not last, whereas the latter is established by way of worship, vigilance, and effort. States are granted by grace, while stations are attained through effort. When the state endures, it becomes a station. The way of the station of divine love means to be intimate with God by His grace; he who loves God will see this love become love of everything in existence and no evil or enmity will be mixed with it. My lord al-Junayd said, "The station of love (*maḥabba*) is an outpouring of fervor which is free of distraction." This refers to the fervor of the heart for its Lord, and for what will cause it to draw near to Him without any wish for reward or recompense. A story of Sufi love comes to us from my father (may God sanctify his secret!) and shows that love for those on the path benefits the lover and transports him from the material to the spiritual world. He said, "There was once in the Maghrib a young saintly woman called al-Manubiyya, whose tomb is well known to this day. One day a rogue saw her and fell in love with her because of her great beauty. Now she used to go out after sunset to visit the tomb of a saint in the desert. The rogue waited until she went out alone so that he could abduct her in the dark. One evening he saw her leave her house and followed her to the place in the desert, thinking that she did not see him, when suddenly he saw two men approaching, dressed all in white. They came towards her with respect, greeted her, and said, 'O noble lady! The saint so-and-so has passed away. Whom do you wish should take his place and hold his spiritual station and function?' The lady turned to where the rogue was lying concealed among the rocks, and pointed towards him. 'I wish that this rogue take his place.' At that moment the veil was lifted from him and he realized her true nature and her spiritual station. He was seized by a great ecstasy and began to cry out and pray humbly to God to forgive him and accept his repentance. And he became a traveler on the path for the love of God."

The Station of Extinction in God

Shaykh Abd al-Karim al-Qushayri said in his *Risāla*: "There are three degrees of extinction in God: First, extinction of the soul and its qualities, and subsistence of the qualities of God in it. Second, extinction of the qualities of God through pure contemplation of Him. Third, extinction of contemplation of God by complete annihilation in His Being." Professor Abu al-Ala Afifi from the University of Alexandria comments on this in his book, which is a translation from a work by the English orientalist Reynold Nicholson,[95] as follows: "It is strange that these words should come from a Sunni Sufi such as al-Qushayri, for they clearly refer to the doctrine of the oneness of being (*waḥdat al-wujūd*). However, they are significant, for they demonstrate to us the danger we may fall into if we take the Sufi sayings literally and understand only their most outward meaning. In fact, Qushayri meant by what he calls 'annihilation in the Being of God' the Sufi's extinction of his thought and will through contemplation of the divine Being; his annihilation is thus not a conscious act. At times this extinction is accompanied by a state in which the Sufi goes out of his senses, although this is not generally the case."

Spiritual Songs

Through their spiritual songs during sessions of invocation the Sufis become more intimate with their Lord. Some Sufi brotherhoods have even introduced the use of musical instruments into the sessions of prayer. Our *ṭarīqa*, however, uses no instruments, such as tambourines, nor has it any special customs with regard to this. The sessions of prayer include spiritual songs, praises to the Prophet, poetry, and Sufi songs. My father did not permit anyone in the *zāwiya* to sing without having first mastered the fundamental rules of music. In fact we had a special group of men whose duty it was to give the call to prayer and to sing. Anyone who wished to be a singer had to perfect his knowledge of Arabic so as not to commit any errors and had to have a good voice and be able to sing well. Thus the group of singers we had were learned in the science of music and composition and possessed voices known for their beauty. Those Sufis who permit and make use of spiritual songs base their standpoint on written evidence from the past on this subject. In the *Saḥīḥ* of al-Bukhari it states that Ubayd ibn Ismail related from Abu Usama, on the authority of Hisham, on the authority of his father, that Aisha (may God be pleased with her!) said, "Abu Bakr came while I had two slave girls from the Ansar with me. They were singing according to their custom, for that day was one of festivities, but they were not very good singers. Abu Bakr said, 'Are the devil's songs in the house of the Messenger of God, and this on a day of festivities?' The Messenger of God said to him, 'O Abu Bakr! Every people has a form of celebration, and this is theirs.'"

The Invocation

On the subject of invocation Sufism has profound and detailed explanations. Invocation (*dhikr*) in Sufism stands for the refuge the disciple seeks in God, and his standing before God signifies concentration upon Him. The invocation of God is practiced using the supreme Name of the Essence, *Allāh*. There are different modes of remembrance; among them is the outward remembrance (*al-dhikr al-jahri*), which takes place in the sessions of invocation and involves repetition of the Name of Majesty aloud. This type of invocation is considered to be the first stage in the path of the Sufi and its intention is to unite everything and everyone to God. It is like a prayer to call people to come together and perform the act of true remembrance. Then there is the individual invocation (*al-dhikr al-ifrādi*) where the disciple remembers God most high with the Name of the Essence. There are two modes of practicing this invocation: one by pronouncing the Name in a measured way and this is when the disciple repeats the Name of God continuously and habitually without drawing out the syllables. Then there is the prolonged elocution of the Name where the disciple invokes the Name by drawing out the syllable between the second *lam* and the *hā* (*Allāah*). This is the invocation by which the disciple attains victory and is known as the hidden remembrance (*al-dhikr al-khafy*). Moreover, I would say that travel on the path of the Sufis is solely by the drawn-out invocation. The disciple is not permitted to practice this until after he has been initiated into it by an authority in the *ṭarīqa* such as the Shaykh, his representative, or a disciple who has permission to initiate whoever is prepared from among his brethren. Without this permission the disciple will not achieve peace of soul through the invocation, for the invocation may expose him to the divine Lights without being prepared spiritually and psychically to receive them. They will dazzle him and he will not be able to bear them, just as one is dazzled if he suddenly exposes himself to the light of the sun when his eyes are not accustomed to it.

The foundation of the path is the holy Book, the practice of the Prophet, the search for knowledge, and much remembrance of Him in concentration and with an attitude of worship. The essential light of the soul will find its reflection in the light of knowledge and in the light of the invocation for whosoever perseveres in it, until the blemishes and impurities of the soul are expelled and it draws near to the divine Presence. There will then come a point where it is obliterated by His totality and the invocation will burn away everything apart from the One invoked.

The starting point of invocation is contemplation. Contemplation among the Sufis is essential, for it is a form of worship. One should not contemplate the Essence of God, but rather His attributes within existence. Concerning this, Shaykh Muhy al-Din ibn Arabi confirmed that it should not be upon His Essence, but rather one should base oneself in His secondary manifestations—"Contemplate the creation of God, do not contemplate the Essence of God." And he said of the secondary manifestations—"To search for the Essence therein is to associate something with God. Incapacity for realization is itself realization (*al-baḥth ᶜan al-dhāt ishrāk, wa al-ᶜajz ᶜan al-idrāk idrāk*)." The Sufi masters all agree that the servant is incapable of grasping the Essence of God and of comprehending It. This is why they do not practice contemplation of It. The Companions of the Prophet are examples to guide us. It is from them that we have the belief that weakness (*ᶜajz*) itself is the key to attainment. Abu Bakr al-Siddiq was asked: "By what do you know your Lord?" He said, "I know my Lord by my Lord." "And how do you know Him?" He replied, "Inability to realize is itself a realization."

Notes

1. It is said that every age must have a spiritual "pole" to keep the religion alive.

2. XVII, 24.

3. V, 83.

4. See Quran, XLVIII.

5. The Isawiyyah *ṭarīqa* founded by Shaykh Muhammad ibn Isa (d. 1523).

6. Ali, cousin of the Prophet, was heir to his spiritual legacy (translator's note).

7. Where the Shaykh al-Madani's *zāwiya* was, near Tripoli in Libya.

8. *Ḥadīth* transmitted by Umar.

9. The *Ḥikam* of Ibn Ata Illah al-Iskandari, d. 1309.

10. Plural of *faqīr*, lit. "poor," "one in need" of God. The term for a disciple in a *ṭarīqa* (translator's note).

11. XXIV, 36–37.

12. One is the "desirous" the other the "desired" (translator's note).

13. Al-Shadhili.

14. Western North Africa.

15. XXIX, 45.

16. From a *ḥadīth* where the archangel Gabriel asked the Prophet what constitutes *iḥsān*, "excellence," and he replied, "*Iḥsān* is that you worship God as if you saw Him and if you do not see Him, yet verily He sees you."

17. Modern-day Lebanon or Israel.

18. XLVIII, 29.

19. "There is no divinity save God."

20. XXXIII, 41–42.

21. III, 191.

22. XIII, 28.

23. Suyuti, *al-Ṣayf al-Qāṭiᶜ*, p. 16.

24. *Astaghfiru Allāh al-ᶜAẓīm alladhi lā ilāha illa Huwa al-Ḥayy al-Qayyūm wa atūbu ilayh.*

25. *Lā ilāha illa Allāh.*

26. LXXI, 10–12.

27. Shaykh Mustafa Naja, *Kashf al-Asrār*, p. 28.

28. XXXIII, 56.

29. *Kashf al-Asrār*, p. 112.

30. The Jews and Christians (translator's note).

31. Shaykh Ibn Abbad, *al-Mafākhir al-ᶜĀliyya*, p. 181.

32. Ibid., pp. 181–182.

33. Abu Dawud and Bukhari related in the *ḥadīth* literature, and Tirmidhi related in his *Shamāʾil* on the authority of Qayla, daughter of Makrama, that she saw the Prophet (peace and blessings be upon him!) sitting with his legs drawn up. She said: "When I saw the Messenger of God sitting thus with such humility, I trembled from fear."

34. LXII, 26–27.

35. LI, 22.

36. There is another version of this *ḥadīth*: "I was a Prophet when Adam was still between spirit and body." Ahmad and Bukhari narrated it.

37. XII, 53.

38. LXXV, 2.

39. XCI, 8.

40. LXXXIX, 27-30.

41. LV, 46.

42. Silver coin worth twenty piastres (translator's note).

43. Her guardian (translator's note).

44. The direction of Mecca, towards which the Muslim prays (translator's note).

45. A *ḥadīth*, narrated by Tirmidhi in his *Jāmᶜi* in the chapter on Quranic exegesis.

46. January 28, 1899.

47. XVIII, 83.

48. Ataturk's Turkish Nationalist Party which eventually overthrew the caliphate in 1924.

49. XV, 99.

50. The *Ḥikam*, from which Sayyida Fatima has quoted previously (translator's note).

51. Dr. Muhammad Mahmud Ahmad.

52. X, 102.

53. Published by the Imperial Iranian Academy in 1977 from a colloquium held July 22-31, 1973.

54. *Ṭabaqāt al-Awliyāʾ* by Shaykh Abd al-Wahhab al-Shirani, pp. 4–5, and the *Taʾyīd al-Ḥaqiqa al-ᶜĀliyya* of Suyuti, p. 21.

55. *Sharḥ al-Ḥikam al-ᶜAtāʾiyya*, by Ibn Ajibah, p. 8.

56. XXXV, 15.
57. XXVIII, 24.
58. *Laṭā'if al-Minan*, p, 21. The relationship here is clearly to God (translator's note).
59. *Al-Tadbīrāt al-Ilāhiyya bi al-Mamlaka al-Insāniyya* by Muhy al-Din ibn Arabi, from an old manuscript, p. 9.
60. *Risāla* of al-Qushayri, pp. 7–8.
61. *Qawā'id al-Taṣawwuf* by Ahmad Zarruq, p. 33.
62. II, 269.
63. *Ḥadīth* (translator's note).
64. *Qawā'id al-Taṣawwuf*, p. 2.
65. *Ta'yīd*, p. 52, and *Taᶜarruf*, p. 14.
66. Al-Kalabadhi, d. 990.
67. *Ta'yīd*, p. 53, and *Taᶜarruf*, p. 21.
68. Al-Kalabadhi.
69. *Ta'yīd*, pp. 72, 73, 74.
70. XXXVIII, 164.
71. *Ta'yīd*, pp. 76, 77.
72. Meaning the relationship of the Messenger of God to his Lord, he who is His servant and His Messenger (*ᶜabduhu wa rasūluhu*).
73. *Qawā'id*, p. 25.
74. I, 4.
75. I, 4-5.
76. I, 7.
77. LXXXIX, 27, 28.
78. d. 857.
79. d. c. 1336.
80. *Iḥyā' ᶜUlūm al-Dīn* by al-Ghazali.
81. *Qūt al-Qulūb* by al-Makki, d. 996.
82. d. 998.
83. d. 1269.
84. d. 1050.
85. *Qawā'id*, p. 20.
86. XXXIX, 18.
87. d. 951.
88. Al-Qushayri, *Risāla*, p. 69.
89. By Ibn Ata Allāh (translator's note).
90. 1421 A.D.
91. *Ḥadīth.*

92. *Al-Mafākhir al-ʿĀliyya*, p. 136.

93. 1190 A.D.

94. LIII, 42.

95. *Fī al-Taṣawwuf al-Islāmī wa Tārīkhihi: Ṭāʾifa min al-Dirāsāt,* translation with additional comments from the English by R. Nicholson.

Ahmad ben Mustapha al-Alawi (1869-1934)

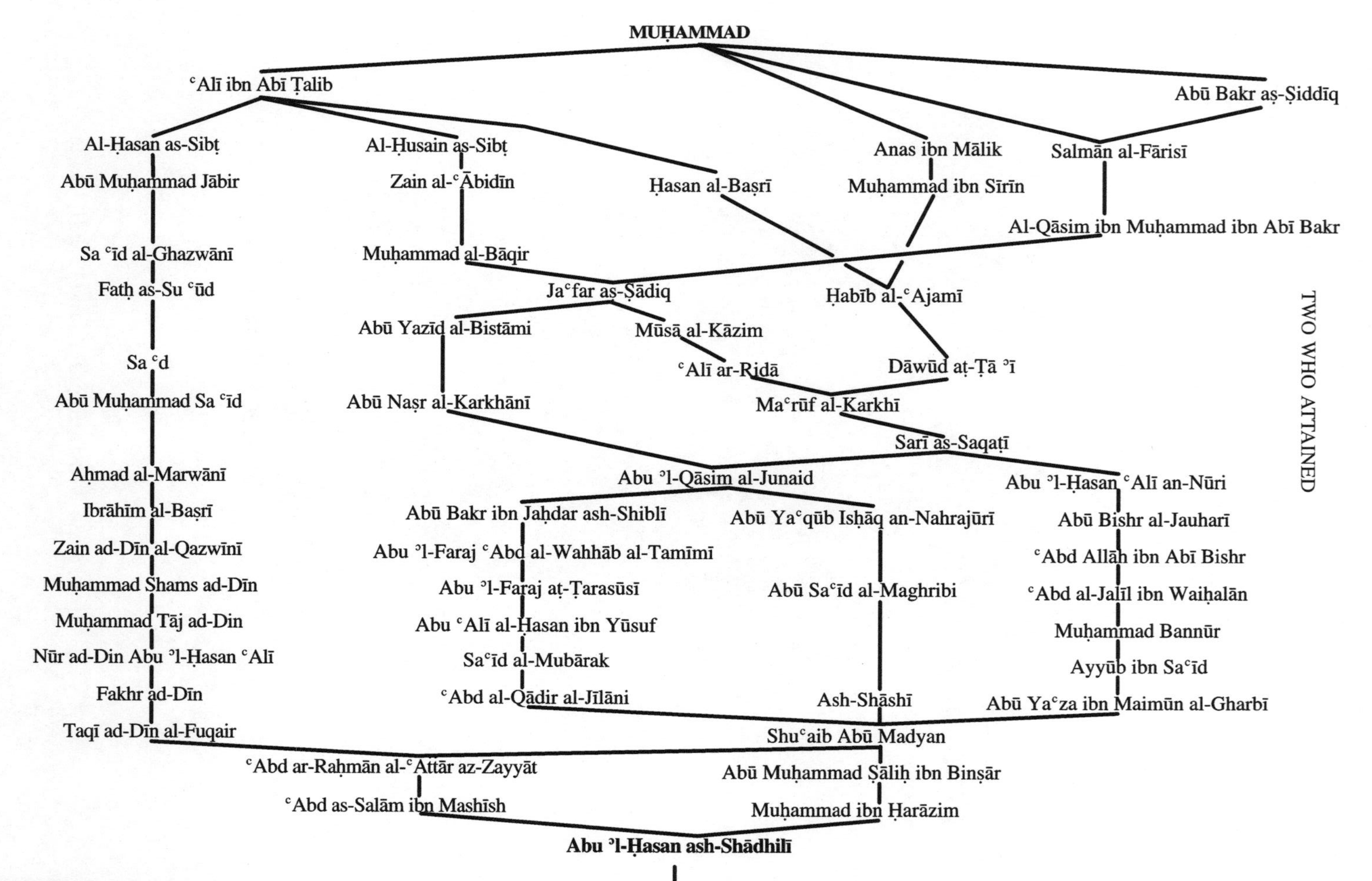
MUḤAMMAD
ᶜAlī ibn Abī Ṭalib
Abū Bakr aṣ-Ṣiddīq
Al-Ḥasan as-Sibṭ
Al-Ḥusain as-Sibṭ
Anas ibn Mālik
Salmān al-Fārisī
Abū Muḥammad Jābir
Zain al-ᶜĀbidīn
Ḥasan al-Baṣrī
Muḥammad ibn Sīrīn
Al-Qāsim ibn Muḥammad ibn Abī Bakr
Sa ᶜīd al-Ghazwānī
Muḥammad al-Bāqir
Fatḥ as-Su ᶜūd
Jaᶜfar aṣ-Ṣādiq
Ḥabīb al-ᶜAjamī
Abū Yazīd al-Bistāmi
Mūsā al-Kāẓim
Sa ᶜd
ᶜAlī ar-Riḍā
Dāwūd aṭ-Ṭā ᵓī
Abū Muḥammad Sa ᶜīd
Abū Naṣr al-Karkhānī
Maᶜrūf al-Karkhī
Sarī as-Saqaṭī
Aḥmad al-Marwānī
Abu ᵓl-Qāsim al-Junaid
Abu ᵓl-Ḥasan ᶜAlī an-Nūri
Ibrāhīm al-Baṣrī
Abū Bakr ibn Jaḥdar ash-Shiblī
Abū Yaᶜqūb Isḥāq an-Nahrajūrī
Abū Bishr al-Jauharī
Zain ad-Dīn al-Qazwīnī
Abu ᵓl-Faraj ᶜAbd al-Wahhāb al-Tamīmī
ᶜAbd Allāh ibn Abī Bishr
Muḥammad Shams ad-Dīn
Abu ᵓl-Faraj aṭ-Ṭarasūsī
Abū Saᶜīd al-Maghribi
ᶜAbd al-Jalīl ibn Waiḥalān
Muḥammad Tāj ad-Din
Abu ᶜAlī al-Ḥasan ibn Yūsuf
Muḥammad Bannūr
Nūr ad-Din Abu ᵓl-Ḥasan ᶜAlī
Saᶜīd al-Mubārak
Ayyūb ibn Saᶜīd
Fakhr ad-Dīn
ᶜAbd al-Qādir al-Jīlāni
Ash-Shāshī
Abū Yaᶜza ibn Maimūn al-Gharbī
Taqī ad-Dīn al-Fuqair
Shuᶜaib Abū Madyan
ᶜAbd ar-Raḥmān al-ᶜAṭṭār az-Zayyāt
Abū Muḥammad Ṣāliḥ ibn Binṣār
ᶜAbd as-Salām ibn Mashīsh
Muḥammad ibn Ḥarāzim
Abu ᵓl-Ḥasan ash-Shādhilī

Abu ʾl ʿAbbās al-Mursī

Aḥmad ibn ʿAṭāʾ Allāh al-Iskandarī

Dāwūd ibn Bākhilī

Muḥammad Wafā Baḥr aṣ-Ṣafā

ʿAlī ibn Wafā

Yaḥya al-Qādirī

Aḥmad al-Ḥaḍramī

Aḥmad Zarrūq

Ibrāhīm al-Faḥḥām

ʿAlī aṣ-Ṣanhājī ad-Dawwār

ʿAbd ar-Raḥmān al-Majdhūb

Yūsuf al-Fāsī

ʿAbd ar-Raḥmān al-Fāsī

Muḥammad ibn ʿAbd Allāh

Qāsim al-Khaṣṣāṣī

Aḥmad ibn ʿAbd Allāh

Al-ʿArabī ibn ʿAbd Allāh

ʿAlī al-Jamal

Al-ʿArabī ibn Aḥmad ad-Darqāwī

Muḥammad ibn ʿAbd al-Qādir — Abū Yaʿza al-Muhājī — Muḥammad ibn Hamza Ẓāfir al-Madanī

Muḥammad ibn Qaddūr al-Wakīlī

Muḥammad ibn al-Ḥabīb al-Būzīdī

Aḥmad ibn Muṣṭafa al-Alawī

ʿAlī Nūr ad-Dīn al-Yashrūṭī

Sayyidah Fatimah Yashrutiyyah

Selected Bibliography

Al-Alawi, Shaykh Ahmad ibn Mustafa:

—*Al-Minaḥ al-Quddūsiyya fī Sharḥ al-Murshid al-Muᶜīn bi tarīq al-Ṣūfiyya.* Written in 1904 but not published until 1941.

—*al-Qawl al-Muᶜtamad fī Mashrūᶜiyyaal-Dhikr bi al-Ism al-Mufrad.* 1927.

Arberry, A. J. *Discourses of Rumi.* London. 1961.

Burckhardt, Titus:

—*An Introduction to Sufi Doctrine.* Thorsons, 1976.

—*Fez, City of Islam.* Islamic Texts Society, 1992.

—*Letters of a Sufi Master.* Translation from the writings of Mulay al-Arabi al-Darqawi. Fons Vitae, Louisville, KY, USA.

Danner, Victor. *Ibn Ata Allah's Sufi Aphorisms.* Brill, 1973. A translation of the *Kitāb al-Ḥikam.*

Ibish, Yusuf, and Peter Lamborn Wilson. *Traditional Modes of Contemplation and Action.* Imperial Iranian Academy, 1977.

Lings, Martin:

—*A Sufi Saint of the Twentieth Century.* London, 1971.

—*What is Sufism*? London, 1975.

Massignon, Louis. *Essai sur les origins du lexique technique de la mystique musulmane.* Paris, 1954.

Michon, Jean-Louis. *Le soufi marocain Ahmad ibn Ajiba et son mi'raj*. Librairie Philosophe, 1973.

Nicholson, R. A. *The Mystics of Islam*. London, 1975.

Nwiya, Paul. *Ibn Ata Allah et la naissance de la confrerie sadilite*. Beirut, 1972.

Schuon, Frithjof:
—*Understanding Islam*. Baltimore, Maryland, 1972.
—*Dimensions of Islam*. London, 1970.
—*Sufism: Veil and Quintessence*. World Wisdom Books, 1981.

Smith, Margaret. *Rabia the Mystic and Her Fellow Saints in Islam*. Cambridge University Press, 1928.

Waddy, Charis. *The Muslim Mind*. New York, 1976.

Al-Yashrutiyya, Fatima:
—*Riḥla ila al-Ḥaqq*. Beirut, 1954.
—*Maṣīratī fī Tarīq al-Ḥaqq*. Beirut, 1981.
—*Nafaḥāt al-Ḥaqq*. Beirut, 1963.
—*Muwāhib al-Ḥaqq*. Beirut, 1966.

Translator's Biography

Leslie Cadavid began her work with the Arabic language at the age of 16, when she moved with her family to Egypt. Upon graduation from high school she attended London University's School of Oriental and African Studies, majoring in Classical Arabic and Islamic Art. She obtained her Bachelor of Arts degree after transferring to Indiana University in 1987, with a major in Near Eastern Languages and Cultures. Her love of Islam and Sufism are the motivations for her work in translation, a work that spans many years and much research.

Index

A

Abraham 207
Acre xiv, xix, 107, 117, 119, 170
Adam 25
Adawiyya, Rabia xix
Shaykh al-Alawi xii
Aleppo 119
al-Arabi al-Darqawi xx
Azhar University 179

B

al-Balāgh al-Jazā᾽iri xvi
Banzart 107, 110
baqā᾽ 7
barzakh 21
Basri, Hasan xix
Beirut 119
Bizerta 107
Burckhardt, Titus xiii
Buzidi, Muhammad xiv

D

Damascus 119, 164, 182
dhikr xiii, xviii, 218

F

fanā᾽ 7, 18, 34, 186
al-Farid, Umar ibn 2, 175, 191

G

ghafla xiii
al-Ghazali 59, 60, 193

H

Haifa 119
al-Hallaj xii
ḥaqīqa xii, 183, 190

I

Ibish, Yusuf 180
Ibn Ajiba 5, 59, 214
Ibn Arabi xx, 119, 172, 178, 186, 195, 207, 219
Ibn Ashir xv
Ibn Ata Allah al-Iskandari 136, 162
iḥsān xi, 30
īmān 26, 30

J

Jaffa 119
Jerusalem 119
Jili, Abd al-Karim 141
Jonah 117
Joseph 24, 25, 26

L

Lings, Martin xxv

M

al-Madani xx
ma῾rifa 203
maḥabba xxi
Mahmud, Abd al-Halim 179
Michon, Jean-Louis xx
al-Minaḥ al-Quddūsiyya xiv, xv

Mostaganem xiv
Muhammad ibn Hamza Zafir al-Madani 112
al-Murshid al-Muᶜīn xv

N

nafs 213
Nasr, Hossein 177
Nwiya, Paul 176

O

Omar ibn al-Farid 2, 191

Q

al-Qawl al-Muᶜtamad fī Mashrūᶜiyya al-Dhikr bi al-Ism al-Mufrad xvi

R

Rhodes 120

S

Safad 119
Salih 117
Schuon, Frithjof xvii, xxi
Shadhili, Abu al-Hasan xii, xiv, xix, 116, 125, 179, 195, 202, 204
sharīᶜa xii, 2, 183
Sidon 119
Smith, Dr. Margaret 175
soul, seven levels of 137

T

takīya 121
tawḥīd 8, 134, 199, 203
Tripoli 119
Tunis 107, 110

W

Waddy, Charis 176
wilāya xii

Y

Yashruti, Ali Nur al-Din xix, 107

Z

zāwiya 121, 164, 165